HERITAGE OF REVIVAL

– *A Century of Rural Evangelism* –

Colin N. Peckham

HERITAGE OF REVIVAL

THE STORY
OF
'THE FAITH MISSION'

ACKNOWLEDGMENT

My thanks are due to the Faith Mission Council for granting me the opportunity and privilege of conducting this research and to my family for bearing patiently with me while I did it. In particular I would like to thank Mr John G. Eberstein MA and Mr Albert Dale who have helped sort out the many details and have given advice concerning the sequence of events and structure of the book. I am also grateful to Mrs Mary McBride, a former pilgrim in Ireland, for typing (and retyping!) so much of the manuscript.

Rev C. N. Peckham BA MTh
Principal
The Faith Mission Bible College

DEDICATED TO
THE PILGRIMS

Preface

The Faith Mission is an interdenominational evangelistic society which was founded in Glasgow in 1886 by John George Govan for the evangelization of the country districts of Scotland. It was born in prayer and as it developed in the atmosphere and experience of true revival it quickly spread over much of Scotland and Ireland and later to parts of England. Particularly in the early years but repeatedly throughout its history there have been blessed movements of the Spirit of God.

Young people were trained in its Bible College in Edinburgh and they moved into the rural areas of the land experiencing the glorious blessing of God as they preached the life-transforming message of the gospel. Now it can look back over 100 years of fruitful harvesting which God has so signally blessed with His presence and power.

The following pages are but a very limited account of its history. So much more could have been written! Thrilling stories of God's saving power in the volumes of magazines and piles of circular letters have reluctantly been laid aside.

The writer trusts that something of the spirit of this pilgrim band has been able to shine through the pages of this little volume. It is the spirit of total involvement, of utter dedication, of willing sacrifice, of complete dependence, of unyielding determination, of saving faith. It is the story of burning words from burning hearts, of that divine unction resting strangely upon one meeting after another. May God preserve this precious quality and lead the Faith Mission into the next century from victory to victory, clothed in the glory of His manifest presence.

May God use this book to quicken our desires and create prayer interest in revival until it comes. May He also use it to stir young people and to thrust them out into God's great harvest field.

Edinburgh   C. N. Peckham
November 1985

Foreword

When Dr Luke wrote his prologue to what we now call 'the Acts of the Apostles' or better still, 'the Acts of the Holy Spirit', he tells us that his 'former treatise' concerned 'all that Jesus *began* . . . to do and teach'. The language suggests that Christ's work did not end with His earthly ministry. Through the Holy Spirit and His church, our risen Lord continues what He commenced on earth. While Luke's historical narrative is part of God's infallible Word, his style of reporting has encouraged similar records of what the Lord Jesus is still doing and teaching today. This is what *Heritage of Revival* is all about. It is 'the Lord's doing', throughout 100 years, 'and it is marvellous in our eyes' (Mark 12:11).

With a host of well-wishers, I rejoice in the work of The Faith Mission for several reasons. The Faith Mission is a *biblical* ministry. The danger of any Christian endeavour is to move from experience to Scripture, instead of from Scripture to experience. Starting with the founder, John George Govan, in 1886, and the pilgrims that have followed in his footsteps, the *motto* of the Mission has been 'Seek first the kingdom of God and His righteousness', and the *message* of the Mission has been 'the whole counsel of God'. This is why the Bible College was established in process of time, and this is why I pray that until Jesus comes again it will continue to be a *Bible* College! Nothing will ever substitute for the anointed exposition of God's Word to meet the basic need of the human heart.

The Faith Mission is a *spiritual* ministry. While every form of evangelism has been pursued for a century, heaven-sent revival has been the prayer-burden of the pilgrims. It is more than edifying; it is exciting to read of past revivals in Fife, the Lothians, and the surrounding areas: revivals in Scotland, revivals in England, revivals in Ireland, the Lewis Awakening, and more. That God would work again in this fashion is the heart-throb of this book (see Chapter 24). With the prophet, we need to cry: 'Oh, that You would rend the heavens! That You would come down! That the mountains might shake at Your presence – As fire burns brushwood, As fire causes water to boil – To make Your name known to Your adversaries, That the nations may tremble at Your presence!' (Isaiah 64:1–2, NKJV). Isaiah knew that mountains would shake and nations would tremble when God came down in demonstration of the Spirit and power.

History confirms this. The average man is not impressed by publicity and programmes, but he is arrested when he sees the supernatural change that God can effect in the lives of men and women. This was so evident in the revivals under Charles Finney. An awareness of God would take hold of a town or city, and under the pressure of the divine presence and the conviction of the Holy Spirit, men and women would fall to the ground and cry for mercy. Soon awe and fear came on the whole community. God used this means to awaken the indifferent and cynical who had sat unmoved for years under the preaching of the gospel. When revival truly affects God's people inexplicable things begin to happen. In the words of Jonathan Edwards: 'When the Holy Spirit sets in, as much is done in a few days as at ordinary times in a year or two'.

The Faith Mission is a *practical* ministry. As you read through the pages of this book, you will be impressed with the aspects and avenues of Christian service. These pilgrims of the past knew what Paul meant when he declared, 'I have become all things to all men, that I might by all means save some' (1 Corinthians 9:22, NKJV). Whole chapters are given to ways of winning men and women, boys and girls, to the Saviour: school sessions, film showings, field meetings, children's camps, literature displays, Christian bookshops, house-to-house visitation, open air work, church services, deeper life conventions – and the list goes on.

My wife, Heather, had an aunt who was a Faith Mission pilgrim. Her name was Doris Brown. So holy was her life, and so fruitful was her service for Christ that Heather, as a teenager, cherished a holy ambition to be like Aunt Doris – bonnet and all! 'With all her spirituality', my wife recalled, 'she was so practical and considerate of others'. Doris was 'called home' in the very act of preaching.

Many have paid tribute to the Faith Mission; indeed, some are mentioned in these pages, such as the Reverend Bertie Rainsbury, Dr J. G. S. S. Thomson, Dr Graham Scroggie, the Reverend Duncan Campbell, and others. I feel honoured to add my name to this illustrious list on this anniversary occasion. I do so in the earnest hope that the story of 100 Years of Rural Evangelism will inspire a new generation to 'become "pilgrims on the earth"', and trust God with their future, as well as the present'.

Thomas Goodwin aptly distinguished our mission as pilgrims here on earth when he observed that 'God had only one Son and He made Him a preacher'. Let us likewise 'Preach the word! . . . [and] do the work of an evangelist' (2 Tim. 4:2, 5, NKJV). The call is clear:

> Rise up, O men of God!
> Have done with lesser things;
> Give heart and soul and mind and strength
> To serve the King of kings.

Stephen F. Olford, President
Encounter Ministries, Inc.

Contents

'THE CHIEF'
JOHN GEORGE GOVAN

CHAPTER 1

Beginnings

'The Faith Mission started.' These simple words were jotted down in the little black diary. The date was 14th October, 1886, and the writer was twenty-five year old John George Govan from Glasgow.

'The Reaper,' a monthly periodical of the day, reported in the November 1886 issue:

> 'We are greatly pleased to hear from our friend, Mr John George Govan, that he has originated a "Faith Mission", for sending out preachers to "the villages and small towns of Scotland". The preachers are not to be guaranteed any salary, nor are subscriptions to be asked, as it is believed "The Lord will provide". Operations have already commenced . . .'

In the December issue, 'The Reaper' reported the requirements and emphasis of the newly founded 'Faith Mission':

> 'Only men and women "full of faith", and of the Holy Spirit (Acts 6:5) are wanted for this work, who will trust their Father to fulfil His promises by supplying them with food, clothing and all the necessaries; who are willing to lose their lives for Christ's sake and the Gospel's, and who, laying aside earthly ambitions, and "seeking not their own", are willing to become "Pilgrims on the earth", and trust God with their future as well as with the present. Further, only those are desired who know what it is to have received the fullness of the Holy Spirit since they believed, who have experienced in their hearts and lives the cleansing and sanctifying power of the Spirit, and who, because the Holy Spirit has come upon them, have power to be God's witnesses, are set at liberty from formality

1

and the fear of man, and are consequently in a position to declare the truth with all boldness.'

Unquestionably the demands of the new work were exacting. Workers were called to turn from the world, its allurements of wealth, its security of employment, its honour of position. Said John George, 'I can never thank God enough for showing me how little were earthly gains, honours and pleasures compared with getting souls saved'. In a statement drawn up in the first few weeks of the Mission he wrote, 'We want those who will forswear all comforts of home, all the ambitions of life and the pleasures of the world to go out as "pilgrims and strangers on the earth", and live entirely for God'. The motto of the Mission, 'Seek first the Kingdom of God and His righteousness', was to be the basic premise upon which the Mission was launched.

The first few workers joined him and, over the years, the vision of a Christ who left the Throne of Glory to die for sinful men has inspired young people to action. Hours spent in idle amusement have been swept away by a flood of spiritual activities. The spirit of abandonment to Christ has replaced attitudes of ease and comfort and propelled them forward. They had to speak! Not to do so would be to deny the very nature of the indwelling Saviour. These young people were born to reproduce. That was the purpose of their existence. The love of Christ constrained them. They would say with Jeremiah, 'The word is in my heart like a burning fire shut up in my bones. I am weary of holding it in; indeed I cannot'. (Jer 20:9 NIV); and with Amos, 'The Lord God hath spoken, who can but prophesy?' (Amos 3:8). They were called to 'shew forth the praises of Him' who called them 'out of darkness into His marvellous light' (I Pet 2:9). The life of the Spirit surging within them demanded expression, revelation, reproduction! They were persuaded by the Scriptures, stimulated by the very nature of the Church, inflamed by the sacrifice of Calvary, convinced by the need of sinful men, compelled by the responsibility to tell the lost, constrained by the Spirit, urged on by the love of Christ, stirred by the coming Judgement, mastered by the commission of Christ – and they went!

Young people with burning hearts, young people whose lives God had touched, young people who were one in purpose and service, became the vehicles of vision, the instruments of illumination, the medium of the manifestation of God's great love. They united to do battle for their King, to do exploits for their God.

That first little group joined hands with their youthful leader, and stepped out into a world which was both hostile and apathetic, to preach in no uncertain terms the Gospel which saves from sin. War was declared against evil. The Faith Mission was launched.

Of course, dedication of this kind costs. John George Govan himself paid the price. He said, 'It meant a great deal to me, in my experience, when I was taken to pieces, bit by bit, by the Holy Spirit. It took weeks and months, and it was when I was willing to lay at His feet *everything* – desires, ambitions, affections – that the blessing came. It means the cross. There is a continual cry to us to come down from the cross; but if we do come down to the care of what others say, we lose the power. If there is no cross, there is no power. We are called to sacrificial service, and to have fellowship with the sufferings of Christ'.

He, and the others of that little group of young people, embraced the cross, and knew, in those early meetings, a 'tremendous consciousness of the glory and presence and power of the living Christ with us'.

With singleness of purpose and total abandon, they threw themselves into the work of God, losing their lives for the salvation of others. Dr Graham Scroggie commented in 1950 that 'throughout two generations, and over wide areas, they have lit the fires of revival'.

Now we look back over the faith that spans a century, over

one hundred years of rural evangelism and Christian service. There has been a great deal of sheer hard work. There have been the hours of faithful visiting, the demands of constantly meeting people, the responsibility of the preparation and preaching of sermons. There have been the thousands of open-air meetings, conferences and conventions. There has been the formation of prayer groups, the establishment of a Training Home and Bible College, and that of district headquarters. A literature department disseminating large quantities of Christian literature from its fourteen shops is operating effectively. There have been the extended times of prayer. There has been the song of triumph when God swept to victory in one campaign after another. This has been happening for a century, and, thank God, it is still happening.

It is with a sense of awe and wonder that we read of the revivals that were the hall-mark of those early pilgrim days, and which have been experienced periodically throughout the century.

It is with gratitude that we too have sensed in some small measure the throb of spiritual power in gatherings in our own day. As we survey this godly heritage, we stand in amazement, humility and praise to God that He should have used this humble channel for the salvation and blessing of so many throughout the century.

CHAPTER 2

Scotland Before 1886

What was Scotland like in the latter part of the nineteenth century? Was the beginning of The Faith Mission an isolated event, separated from the general trend of things, or was it part of a wide-spread movement of the Spirit of God throughout the country?

The year 1843 was the year of the great schism in the national Church in Scotland when many protested against the 'intolerable bondage' of State interference in religious affairs. It was known as 'The Disruption', for over 470 ministers withdrew from the Established Church to form the Free Church of Scotland. Their action profoundly moved the nation, as they lost their homes and their endowment. Many of the ablest men seceded and those of deep religious faith followed them. Only 729 ministers remained in the National Church. During the next two years 500 places of worship were built and opened.

The ten years following the Disruption may be described as a period of almost complete reconstruction in the church fabric in Scotland. It took at least that time for the Established Church to recover from the shock that had threatened her very existence, and for the Free Church to build up an organization that covered the land. Gradually the acute crisis settled down to a course of normal development.

On the other hand the United Presbyterian Church was formed in the union of two bodies which had previously left the Church of Scotland. In May 1847 the Union of a total of 518 congregations took place.

Three great bodies now divided the country with persistent rivalry between them. While there were strong differences, the very superabundance of religious facilities fostered an intensity for evangelical truth.

Between 1858 and 1861 a wave of revival swept the USA and was experienced in Britain, mainly in Ireland and to a lesser extent in Scotland and England. In Scotland all the churches felt the breath of new life to a greater or lesser degree.

The battle for reunion now engrossed the minds of church leaders, and for years anti-union agitation clashed with the promoters of union. Poor Scotland, rent asunder by divisions, with no idea of how to bridge the serious rifts which so deeply divided the people. Onto this saddened and confused scene strode a man who was destined to write his name permanently into Scottish history, the American evangelist, D. L. Moody.

On 17th June 1873 Moody, three years younger than C. H. Spurgeon, slipped unobtrusively into Liverpool with the singer Ira D. Sankey. Unknown, and almost uninvited, they at first had difficulty in finding a place in which to minister. Moody had allocated six months to Britain, and despite good meetings, the tour was in danger of fizzling out. At this point he received an invitation to go to Edinburgh from a committee representative of Free and Established churches. He went. On 23rd November 1873 the Edinburgh campaign began. How would Edinburgh react to these two breezy Americans? Moody's English was atrocious and his racy torrent of anecdote and informal Bible teaching might shock and irritate the grave, rigid and theologically educated Scots. Scotland, weakened by the Disruption, wore a cloak of piety and good conduct, but joy and religion were divorced, and many even thought it blasphemy to claim certainty of heaven. Stiff, credal orthodoxy was absolutely in possession. Scots had long been nurtured on the solemn creeds and dogma of historic Christianity. For centuries their minds had been drilled in the Shorter Catechism and the doctrines of the Westminster Confession, even where no Christian experience was to be found. The worship of the Scottish Church had been conducted on rigidly Puritan lines.

Strong feelings existed against the use in services, of 'human' hymns and for the most part only the Psalms were sung. The battle to introduce the organ into public worship only began in 1856, and for the next ten years debates as to its use continued in parish churches and Assembly halls. To bring Sankey, with his 'kist o' whustles', as his little harmonium was called, and with his Gospel songs to this country, and to its capital city – well!

Moody came, however, to an audience prepared for him. 'What is prayer?' he asked rhetorically at a children's meeting. He paused, not anticipating an answer, but hundreds of young voices surprised him by responding in unison. 'Prayer is an offering up of our desires unto God, for things agreeable to His will, in the Name of Christ, with confession of our sins, and thankful acknowledgement of His mercies.' He did not know that he had asked a question from the Shorter Catechism. He and Sankey put a match to the well-laid dry sticks of Scottish religion. They did more.

With no ecclesiastical credentials these two unknown American evangelists were used by God to lift the country above its sectarian divisions and rifts. Dimly, after weary years of wrangle, Scotland perceived that the road to unity lay in the realm of devotion to Christ by personal commitment and Christian service. What discussion and argument had failed to do, two strangers from America had done. They eliminated to a large extent the bitter division in the country. A warmth and a kindness grew between ministers of different denominations as had not been experienced before. Stiff conservative Edinburgh took from two unaccredited American evangelists what they never would have taken from their own kith and kin. Edinburgh turned out to hear the evangelists, and in the five-week mission about 3,000 people were brought into the Kingdom. Moody, thirty-six years old, swept from obscurity to fame.

After three weeks in Dundee, they came to Glasgow and

began on 8th February 1874. Week after week the meetings continued in churches and halls. To these meetings the people came from shipyards and mills, from grimy tenements and sumptuous houses.

Moody's meetings were the subject of conversation everywhere. On one occasion in the Botanical Gardens, Moody preached to between 20,000 and 30,000 people. Glasgow was conquered. Another 3,000 men, women and children sought the Saviour. Through the whole of 1874 revival burned over a Scotland which now numbered 3½ million. Men bowed before the wind of the Spirit as it swept across the country. These were days of Scotland's spiritual visitation. Andrew Murray of South Africa returning to Scotland a few years after Moody's visit, noticed that 'the whole religious tone of Scotland had been brightened most remarkably'.

Then followed a surge of activity, spiritual and social, through avenues old and new. The United Evangelistic Committee which brought Moody to Glasgow perpetuated itself as the Glasgow Evangelistic Association to begin a long, honourable career in evangelism and philanthropy – Poor Children's Day Refuges, Temperance Work, Fresh Air Fortnights, the Cripple Girls' League, the Glasgow Christian Institute, and a tent on the Glasgow Green where a free breakfast was served weekly.

Eight years later Moody visited Scotland again. He spent six weeks in Edinburgh, and, early in 1882 five months in Glasgow. This again produced another out-burst of popularity. Again the blessings of God flowed. John George Govan was able to attend about forty of these meetings and was profoundly moved by them. The Spirit of God seemed to be poured out during this whole period of history, and from this awakening flowed blessings throughout the country and to the ends of the earth.

The Orphan Homes of Scotland were founded in 1872 by William Quarrier. The Boys' Brigade was founded in Glasgow in 1883 by Sir William Smith, a Scot from Thurso. It now has 370,000 boys and 52,000 leaders in its worldwide membership. The Girls' Brigade with a world membership of 182,000, now operating in fifty countries, was founded in 1893.

The Christian Endeavour founded in USA in 1881 came to Britain in 1887 and took deep root. The Annual Glasgow Convention for the Deepening of Spiritual Life began in 1882. The Ayrshire Christian Union was founded in 1878. The African Evangelistic Mission based in Scotland to operate in West Africa was founded in 1888. Christian Unions in various parts of the country sprang up, all active in evangelism, and zealous for true godliness. They emerged in Lanarkshire, Renfrewshire, Galloway, Perthshire, Forfar and Clackmannanshire. The Duns and Tillicoultry Evangelistic Associations were formed at this time.

The Glasgow Railway Mission was founded in 1885. The Scottish Home Mission to the Jews was founded in 1885. The Paisley Lodging House Mission was founded in 1887. The Mission to Lepers in India with its secretary in Edinburgh began in 1875. The Glasgow University Students' Christian Association was founded in 1886. The Salvation Army began in Scotland in 1882. The Mission to Deep Sea Fishermen was founded in 1883. The League of Prayer was founded in England in 1891. The Keswick Convention began in 1875. The Bible Training Institute in Glasgow opened in 1893.

Service for Christ flowed from a quickened and an awakened people. Scotland was alive to God and His working. It was at this time of spiritual awakening and evangelistic fervour that the Faith Mission was born. It was not an isolated happening. It was part of a spiritual awakening which moved across the country stirring Christians, saving sinners, transforming communities.

Christian young people were able and mobile. They needed an avenue through which they could express God's love to men, and God brought the Faith Mission into being to fulfil His purposes. It was born in a country which was soaked in scripture and biblical teaching, in an atmosphere of prayer, and in the spirit of revival. A work had begun in a land which was ready for a clear, simple and decisive Gospel message.

Unlike the large towns and cities, the country districts did not have many privileges in the evangelistic field, and it was to these that the pilgrims were drawn. They went out with few earthly possessions giving themselves wholeheartedly and sacrificially, enduring all sorts of difficulties and hardships, sensing only the compulsion of the Spirit, and they found that God was with them, working mightily to the salvation of many men and women.

CHAPTER 3

A Young Man is Prepared

Who was John George Govan, and how did the Faith Mission begin? Born on the 19th January 1861, he was the fourth son and tenth member in a family of twelve. The father, William Govan, a prominent Glasgow merchant, followed in the footsteps of his father, well-known in the cotton industry, and established a large weaving factory at Pollokshaws. William Govan was a godly man, a faithful witness for Christ, and when elected to the Glasgow Town Council, threw his considerable influence behind the temperance movement and all social and moral reforms.

The family lived in a large stone house called 'Southpark' in Hillhead, in the West End of Glasgow. It was a happy, well disciplined home with the Bible being read both mornings and evenings. Every sort of worldly amusement and all questionable pursuits were denied to the children, yet many wholesome pastimes were provided. Five of the six boys became preachers and writers and each of the sisters, attractive Christian women.

At the age of twelve, the Spirit of God began to move in the heart of John George. When on holiday with the family on the Island of Arran, his father's preaching on the rocks at Corrie on a summer's Sunday evening brought conviction to his heart. That evening, alone in his little room with the skylight window, he trusted Christ for forgiveness and for eternal life. Testimony was not encouraged in those days and although he attended meetings at school and in his home circle, his Christian experience was erratic and half-hearted. He was inclined to be moody and self-willed, proud and sensitive but never lost the assurance of sins forgiven. He was a Sunday

11

School teacher, 'but this was more a matter of duty than of interest', he said. 'Any earnestness I had was fluctuating, and my mind was worldly.'

In 1882 Moody and Sankey paid their second visit to Glasgow. The six-month mission began three days after John's twenty-first birthday. Bailie William Govan was closely associated with them and John attended about forty of the gatherings. 'These meetings greatly stirred me', he said, 'and for the first time I began to speak to people about their souls, and to feel my need of spiritual blessing.' Several of his friends were saved, and then his brother James, two years older than he was spiritually transformed. He opened a mission hall at Pollokshaws and walked the five miles to it, often with John George, every Sunday. James' life was radiant and contrasted vividly with that of John George who remarked sadly, 'Other "lords" had dominion over me – worldly ambition, evil temper, pride, the fear of men. I was more influenced by the fear of men than the fear of God, more influenced by the love of men's approval than the love of God's approval'. Such was the power of the life and ministry of his brother James, however, that when D. L. Moody came into contact with him, in 1883, he said to his father, 'Mr Govan, I wish I had a son like that boy of yours'. His life could not be discounted. It was irresistibly attractive and his testimony burned its way into John's heart.

One night at Pollokshaws hall when John was battling with his need of a holy life, his brother James asked him to close in prayer. 'I felt I had to decide there and then. Either I must refuse to pray, or I must trust the Lord to give me the blessing of a clean heart as I prayed. It happened in almost an instant . . . I went down on my knees and prayed, yielding my all to God, and trusting Him to cleanse me there and then. I came out from the meeting, and said to my friend, "I have a clean heart; I trusted the Lord, and I know He has done it for me, though I do not feel any different". When I got home that night and went down before the Lord, then I knew the difference. The glory of God flooded my soul and it has been different ever since.'

His life was transformed, and he entered into joyful service, first among the factory girls at Pollokshaws, and then, together with others, in one of Glasgow's worst and most needy districts – Water Street. Almost every night they were involved, with four or five meetings on Sundays. 'We were desperate about sinners!' he exclaimed. They met in a hall in Water Street, and it was this area which gave them the training for effective work in later years. The greatest impression left upon him from those early days was 'the amount of time we gave to prayer. Prayer became a great joy. We delighted in it . . . Whole nights of prayer were then our experience, and many of our Saturday afternoons were given to prayer'.

It was at this time that he sensed the need to be endued with power for service even more so than that which he was already experiencing. He trusted God to fill him with His Spirit, and God 'revealed Himself as the God of love and power, in a way that I never thought possible to the soul of man'. God was preparing His young servant both practically and spiritually for the task of which he was at that stage totally unaware.

Although he enjoyed the business world, the time had come when he could no longer continue in it, for the work of God demanded his full attention. One day he was watching, from the hilltops above Corrie on the Island of Arran, the pleasure yachts flitting about on the blue waters of the Firth of Clyde, aimless and purposeless, only bent on pleasure. He saw also the large liners laden deep with the merchandise of nations, purposefully breasting the waves of the great seas, each one with a definite port to reach. The Spirit of God spoke to him there. He might choose to spend his life in prosperous business and plentiful ease, or else he might offer himself, utterly and entirely, body, soul and spirit, to Christ for the carrying of the Gospel message into the much neglected villages and countryside of his native land. He made his choice, the result of which, as the years have passed, has been an ever-widening stream of blessing which has flowed on, reaching to the far corners of the earth.

'I resolved that I would go out and take missions myself . . . My first was at Lochwinnoch, where we had thirty or forty converts in a fortnight. The next call was to a mission at Tarbert, and my third mission was with a friend at Irvine.'

The days of great adventure with God had begun. Irvine was quite remarkable. On the seventh night God broke through and fifty or sixty sought the Saviour. This was the beginnings of 'a revival which went on for nearly a month'. Hundreds of newly converted folk were marching the streets singing and witnessing to their wonderful Lord.

The next place was Stewarton. The youthful preacher, described by one as, 'only a boy', found it 'very stiff'. He spent a day in prayer. 'The whole atmosphere was changed and by the end of the week we had a hundred young people saved and marching the streets, and witnessing in the open-air.'

It is a matter of interest that at about the time of the Stewarton mission a baby boy was born in the home in which John George Govan was given hospitality. We may be sure that this little one was the subject of much prayer at that time. When he grew up he went into the ministry of the Church of Scotland, and throughout his life remained a faithful friend and supporter of the Mission.

The meetings were full of freshness and new life yet the sense of reverence was carefully preserved. Solos and choruses, quite an innovation at that time, were introduced and testimonies abounded. God was in the midst and He was establishing a work to glorify His Name.

John George, together with others, drew up a paper, and discussed the formation of a proposed movement to be called, 'The Scottish Mission and Prayer Union', but it came to nothing. In the autumn of 1886 the principles and ideas which were gripping his mind and life came to fruition in the form of the Faith Mission, 'though there was not much of form or organization about us then', he wrote later.

Something must be done for Scotland! He resolved to ask others to join him and to go out in faith as the China Inland missionaries did, trusting God to supply their needs. Fiery George Colvin joined him, and the first two 'Pilgrims', as the workers were called, set out for the first mission, Colvin to Moffat, and Govan to Whitehaven. The faith principle would now be put to the test. People came to the Saviour at nearly every meeting, with about sixty converted in Whitehaven and good numbers converted in Moffat as well. When they closed, after paying all the fairly considerable expenses, Colvin had one shilling and sixpence, and Govan five pounds. The Faith Mission went ahead entirely on faith lines, and to this day it goes on in the same way. 'We appeal directly to God', said Mr Govan, 'we go on with the work, and God has never failed us.'

Over the years, God has supplied the need in little ways and by large sums. Folk have recognized the spiritual worth of the work and have responded by contributing sums, which on occasions met the need exactly. The Mission is not supported by private means, but each gift is put into soul-saving activity for spiritual and eternal returns.

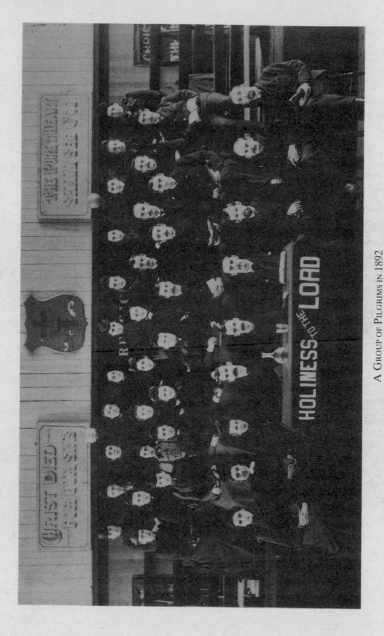

A GROUP OF PILGRIMS IN 1892

Those in the centre in the front row are (left to right) Messrs. P. L. Corsie, J. G. Govan and H. E. Govan. Mr J. B. McLean is fourth from the right in the third row.

CHAPTER 4

Revival at its Roots

After John George Govan and George Colvin had begun the Mission, the next to offer for the work were two young ladies, both of whom had some experience in the work at Pollokshaws and Water Street. It was unusual for women to preach then, and women workers were hardly known outside the Salvation Army. Having seen the effectiveness of the ministry of women in the Salvation Army, and believing that 'your sons and daughters shall prophesy', Agnes Jack and young Annie Martin were accepted as Pilgrims.

Their first mission was at Drymen and they were extremely nervous. At the opening meeting they spoke for three minutes each, but they plodded on with love for God and souls burning in their hearts. Annie Martin wrote, 'About thirty people came every night', and later, 'There were about 200 in the hall'; and later still, 'We had twenty-four converts'. One of those converts from this first mission was a young gamekeeper, James B. McLean who in the years ahead was to become the leader of the work in Ireland.

Then God began to add workers to their number. The glory of God was among them. Earnest devotion, sacrificial living and fervent desire for the salvation of men and women was the hall-mark of these young people.

Those were days when the Spirit of God was being poured out in Scotland. The young workers who were now joining this new Mission were being borne on the crest of a wave of great spiritual power and unction. They were not theologians yet the passion for souls burned within them,

17

and they prayed, and worked and preached with marvellous results. Sinners were swept into the kingdom, lives were transformed and communities were changed.

The secret of it all was the presence of God. The following reports are selected from their letters:

'We have indeed felt the power and presence of God in the meetings. There were two hundred at the meeting last night and we had a glorious time with the Lord. He was present in mighty power. The young men who used to laugh and make a noise are now so solemn.'

'A number of the Peebles converts came down to us here at Inverleithen and gave splendid testimonies. Two lads spoke of being drunkards, but now they are saved and living for God. Hallelujah! At the end eight sought Christ for salvation.'

'God is working mightily here at Killearn. He is pouring out His Spirit. Oh the power of God that souls will be mightily converted and God's Name glorified.'

'At night we had a glorious meeting and forty-one came into the side room and decided for Christ.'

'The Lord is still working here. Souls are being saved every night and the Christians are being stirred up too. Tonight in the after-meeting five souls professed, and afterwards we spoke to the Christians. We had such a blessed time that about twenty consecrated themselves to God. Oh hallelujah! We were so happy that when we came home, we sang praises to Christ, marching around the table! Oh, "How good is the God we adore!" I feel that I can never praise God enough for all that He has done for us.'

'On Saturday we had a grand, hallelujah, free and easy testimony meeting at which a great number testified and at the close of the meeting eight came for Salvation. Bless God!'

'The Lord was present in power. We had a glorious time with the hall packed and a number turning away at the door. What a powerful time with fifteen folk out for Salvation. Praise God!'

'The meeting began at eight and finished at ten-thirty. Great blessing.'

'The work in Walkerburn is getting on splendidly. The hall is quite full every night. Last night twelve came to Christ and eight tonight. Praise God!'

'The hall was packed and some could not get seats. Above all the Lord's Presence was manifest. Had a big after-meeting and fourteen adults and five children professed salvation.'

'The Lord is doing great things here. Last night forty-two came to the Feet of Jesus, but there were a great many more waiting to be spoken to . . . On Friday twenty-two professed and on Saturday after a testimony meeting eighteen gave their hearts to Jesus.'

'With heart and voice we do rejoice in the triumphs of Grace we see around us. Hallelujah! We are on our way to victory. About thirty-six have professed since Thursday. Grand meeting on Saturday, six coming out for God. We had a glorious time on Sunday here at Renfrew. In the forenoon, while I sang "I bring my heart to Jesus", twenty walked right out to the penitent form. Glory be to God! Between crying for joy and shouting hallelujah, I can tell you we had a most blessed time. What must Heaven be like when we are so happy down here! Oh how good of Jesus to use such weak workers of the dust for His glory.'

'We had a prayer meeting from five to six and then marched through the streets till seven. The hall was crowded. McDonald says there were over a thousand, and nineteen came right out for Christ. Hallelujah! I heard of two who trusted Him in their seats, and some decided when they went home, so we don't know the results of the meetings.'

'Last Sunday in the after-meeting twenty-seven boys and girls between the ages of twelve and sixteen, decided for Christ, and fifteen men and women. On Monday we had a grand meeting. The Lord was present in mighty power and six of them decided tonight, yet a great number went away deeply convicted.'

'Yesterday at Irvine we had a powerful meeting. Many could not get in. The Christians say they have never seen such large meetings. Last night there were five hundred present and five adults and three children professed. We had a grand testimony meeting on Saturday, many testifying for the first time. The Christians are getting properly roused up. Miss Girvan was saying that last night's meeting was the largest and most powerful they have ever had – yet we are not satisfied. We want to see people deeply convicted under the Power of God. Oh for a mighty Baptism of the Holy Ghost and of fire.'

Meetings were informal and marches and open-air meetings were organized with blessed results. Sometimes these strange new evangelistic methods were met with opposition from the roughs. The pilgrims and new converts were showered with mud and sometimes stones as they sang and preached. Nothing deterred them, however, and on they would go with the joy of the Lord as their strength. Sometimes it was 'war' when the devil's territory was invaded by these young people who had no reputation to lose, and who only cared about men and women coming to the Saviour. Sometimes it could be a while before they saw a 'break'. 'Keep believing', wrote one, 'the people are beginning to get anxious'.

Testimonies were put to good use in the meetings. 'There were twenty-five good testimonies, and I believe they are the means of much blessing. Many are melted to tears at seeing their old companions testify, and three came out for salvation.'

They rejoiced too that the converts continued to grow in the things of the Lord. 'Most of the converts are very bright; some of the faces are beaming with joy.'

And in the midst of it all how God ministered to their own hearts:

'The Lord has been blessing me wonderfully in my own soul. Sometimes I feel so overcome and so humbled when I think of all my dear Jesus' love and kindness to such an unworthy creature as I am. Oh dear Jesus, just fix our eyes continually on *Thee only* and melt us, and bind us so close to Thy Heart, that we will never, never grieve Thy wondrous love. May we be filled with that boundless love that shall conquer all things.'

'Oh that self was wholly lost in Christ and that we were so taken up with Jesus only that we should not care what others thought about us.'

These were stirring days indeed. At the end of the first year there were nine workers. God had so blessed their labours that about two thousand people had professed faith during that year. In addition He had cared for them and they closed their accounts with £20 in hand!

CHAPTER 5

The Spreading Flame

Fife, and areas of great need north of Edinburgh, were chosen as their focal point of attack during the second year. At Dunfermline for about two weeks not many unconverted came to the meetings. Then about sixty Christians came to a half-night of prayer. 'For fully two hours the Spirit of God searched the hearts of His children, revealing hidden and unclean things, and nineteen came forward and trusted God to cleanse them from all sin. Since then the work has increased with much larger meetings, and conversions take place nightly.' One place after another was 'attacked' and the 'war' was on!

Unforgettable battles there were, both on their knees in the many long periods of prayer, and in the open-air with the roughs doing their utmost to disrupt the meetings and silence the pilgrims. Yet in spite of rotten apples, eggs and mud, victory followed glorious victory in village after village. Hundreds were swept into the Kingdom and this culminated in the great Dunfermline Thanksgiving Demonstration on Saturday 30th June and Sunday 1st July 1888. Prayer Unions had been formed and this was the first anniversary of the inauguration of the Prayer Unions.

People converged on the town from the surrounding areas and combined with the Dunfermline Christians for this exceptional event. Two special trains hired for the purpose brought enthusiastic Christians from towns far and near, and over four hundred streamed from the station platform to the hall, singing rousing hymns as they went. A hall holding 1,500 was filled. At 5 o'clock there was the march of witness when over 800 people marched joyfully down the main streets pouring forth songs of praise to God. What enthusiasm! An astonished clergyman asked, 'Are these all the Lord's people?' The local journal hinted that the only way to glory was via Dunfermline.

The meetings were powerful with stirring testimonies of mighty deliverances followed by dynamic preaching. The Lord was with them in power and thirty Christians rose at the close of the evening meeting to yield to God unreservedly and for ever.

On Sunday in addition to the normal church services which folk were free to attend, there were the Demonstration meetings. Fifteen hundred gathered at the open-air meetings in the park, and hundreds joined the march back to the hall where several responded to the challenge of the great Gospel truths. The blessing was lasting, deep and extensive.

During the eight months in Fife twenty new Prayer Union meetings were formed. Here Christians were able to encourage one another; to have fellowship and to pray with one another, and conserve the work of evangelism. No less than nine Pilgrims joined the Mission from Fife at that time.

One of the great events of those early years was the Rothesay revival. Rothesay is a town on the Isle of Bute on the river Clyde. Pilgrims Martin and Mitchell, 'unassuming young ladies' the papers called them, began meetings on the 20th October 1888. The former wrote at the beginning of the work:

'Throughout the week the meetings have been small, fifty being the largest number present, but praise God we had an attendance of over two hundred last night. We have begun our open-airs. Last night we had a march, and then after the meeting was over we went to the quay head and had a splendid open-air for an hour. Keep praying and believing that the Lord will work mightily here. We got a precious promise this morning that they who wait on the Lord shall be strong and do exploits.'

The 'precious promise' was soon to be a vibrant reality. A further letter, a week later, tells of their progress:

'Hallelujah! Last night we had a glorious meeting. The hall was crammed with four hundred, and five souls professed. The Lord was present in power, and many went away deeply convicted, some with the tears running down their cheeks. Keep believing! We are having splendid open-airs, and last night we had a proper march along the main streets with a great crowd following us!'

So writes the girl who in a few years time would be the wife of John George Govan. Dr Graham Scroggie said of them that they had 'one soul', and surely in these rigorous times she was being prepared for leadership. Rothesay was a place of great opportunity. The two ladies visited, prayed, marched, sang and preached, and the town soon became aware that something significant was happening. The 'fire' was kindling. Weeknight audiences varied from four to eight hundred, and on Sunday nights fifteen hundred or more crowded in from all over the island.

The meetings continued for three months. John George, who was called the Chief (or Chief Pilgrim) was there, and during that time no less than ten pilgrims took part. What times they had! The glory of Heaven filled the place. There were some remarkable cases of conversion. One man with a crutch was a great drunkard and it sometimes took four policemen to hold him. One night coming out of the public house, he was attracted to the open-air by the singing of one of the pilgrims. He went over to her and lifted his crutch to strike her. But the pilgrim sang on and the blow never fell. Later on, that man was soundly converted and bore a wonderful testimony for many years. Hundreds professed conversion during the three months of the mission and eight workers were added to the Mission as a result of the work there.

The influence upon the whole community was such that the

chief magistrate reported that the crime in the town had been greatly diminished that winter, and he attributed this to the work of the Faith Mission. At the close of this mission 260 people united to form a Prayer Union in Rothesay, which for many years was the headquarters of the Mission, and the Rothesay Convention became an annual event. Many could never forget the blessedness of some of those gatherings.

But Rothesay was not the only place in which God was working. The number of pilgrims was increasing and they went everywhere preaching the Gospel. The work spread. There was a wide-spread movement of the Spirit on the Island of Islay. In Bowmore, the chief town, many of the shopkeepers were converted, and commercial travellers would find the shops shut and the people all at the meetings. The halls were crowded, many walked long distances to be present.

Tarbert, Lochgilphead, Inveraray, Kintyre, Campbeltown were all worked. Others were working their way towards Oban, holding missions in the Islands of Luing and Easdale. Oban was reached in 1893 when sister pilgrims held a remarkable mission of three months duration with very blessed results which were felt for many, many years.

The next step was to the Highlands and Islands. The year 1894 was a great year of Faith Mission effort in the Highlands. During the pilgrims' first visit to Ballachulish, near Fort William, in the winter of 1895-96 there was a great revival. The mission lasted four months. At the close of this great move of the Spirit a Prayer Union was formed, and eleven of the early members went into full-time service, the majority spending some time in the Mission.

On they went to the Isle of Mull, the Isle of Tiree and the Isle of Skye. Still further afield, they found themselves on the islands of the Outer Hebrides. By 1898 almost all the islands off the West Coast of Scotland had been visited by the pilgrims. Some islands were very small. In 1902 the pilgrims visited a small island. 'The population was seven families, thirty-nine in all, without a church or chapel, or a missionary. Nearly all of them came to Jesus.'

The self-sacrifice and devotion of the pilgrims in reaching these out of the way places was enormous and they endured much hardness. Travelling or sailing was not luxurious. Pilgrims 'roughed it', and many a tale could be told of the hardships of those days. There was sacrifice, there was suffering, but there were souls to win.

Horace Govan, the younger brother of the Chief, was particularly burdened with the Highlands and Islands and for years he toiled in this area preaching the Gospel, beloved by all.

The Lothians, the area around Edinburgh, was a fruitful field. Revival blessing attended the preaching of the pilgrims as they passed from village to village – with persecutions. In some places revival began the very first night – somebody must have been praying! One said, 'To see big, strong men, as well as women and children weeping their way to Calvary, is a wonderful sight'.

Great joy accompanies revival, and the converts often took their stand immediately in the open-air meetings telling joyfully to those who knew them that Christ had saved and changed them.

Whole villages were brought under conviction of sin. 'Not one man in my bar on a Saturday night', moaned the publican to a policeman, 'and before these meetings the place was packed.' God transformed wild, drinking, swearing men! In some cases the craving for drink was destroyed immediately, in others there was a struggle. One night, a man helplessly drunk was almost carried in by two Christians. They brought him to the penitent form and God saved him. He walked out of the hall erect and sober.

Open-airs were often lively times with heckling and shouting, jeering and yelling to try to break up the meeting. Pilgrims would often go straight for the public house and hold an open-air meeting near to it. They fished where the fish were and sometimes in rough seas!

At the end of the second year there were twenty workers, ten men and ten ladies. Of course it was not all revival. We read that 'attendances at Eaglesham were never very large, and latterly were lessened more by the inclemency of the weather'. 'Some of the missions held this year were quite unsuccessful', writes the Chief. At the close of the fourth year he said, 'there has been no great revival this year, but there has been steady conversion work right through'.

Generally speaking, however, the early years of the Mission were characterized by numerous and blessed movements of the Spirit, the results of which had lasting effects upon one generation after another. The campaigns were not merely the upsurge of evanescent emotion, but moral values and spiritual realities were embraced, and these had eternal benefits for both those who responded and for their children. Families were transformed – for ever.

CHAPTER 6

Early Organization

'We were finding that the converts needed more looking after than we had anticipated', wrote the Chief. In many cases they were not receiving helpful teaching, nor were they being involved in necessary and healthy Christian activity.

The Prayer Unions were increasing with the expanding work. During the first year, twelve were formed, seventeen in the second year, twenty-five in the third, and by the end of the sixth year there were 118 Prayer Unions. All these needed inspiration and encouragement. On occasions weeks of meetings for Christians were held and were blessed to many. Pilgrims sometimes had repeat missions, returning to the same place to teach and stimulate the young converts to consecration and dedicated Christian living. These short visits did much to kindle and fan the flame of divine love and to stir up the work of God, yet more work of this nature was necessary. The work needed care and consolidation.

Pilgrim H. C. M. Patterson was chosen as the first District Pilgrim and he established the first 'District Headquarters' in the home of some friends in Markinch, Fife. From his little attic room he supervised the fourteen Prayer Unions in his charge, visiting regularly, arranging conference meetings and holding gospel meetings where possible. In those days when motor transport did not exist, he walked many miles in this labour of love. On Sundays, in fact, he normally covered thirty-two miles to and from the meetings!

The work was so widespread that more superintending District Pilgrims were needed. Fife and the Lothians, the Highlands and the West Coast, the Border Counties and the South all needed leaders. By 1895 the work in Ireland demanded an appointment as well. The Chief moved around amongst them all, travelling widely and ministering most acceptably in all the fields of the Mission's operations.

'The Chief was a forceful speaker, and at times his speaking had great intensity. Sometimes he used to "catch fire" and his speaking became electrified', recalls Mr Percy Bristow, one-time Secretary and Treasurer of the Mission. 'He would take a passage of Scripture, and when going through it would get inspiration on some thought or word and would catch fire. It was the preaching of a man who had vision.' So this quiet, unpretentious, friendly, burdened man, with qualities of leadership which all acknowledged, moved amongst the Prayer Unions, encouraging, rebuking sin and worldliness in no uncertain terms when necessary, giving wise advice, helping where he could, having the 'care of all the churches'.

He was most meticulous in the administration of the Mission and all records were carefully preserved. Financial matters were scrupulously managed. Letters were answered immediately. He was thoroughly business-like in all his dealings. The Mission had to be run efficiently.

First of all it was administered from Southpark, his home in Glasgow, then after moving several times, the Headquarters was established from 1897 in Rothesay, Isle-of-Bute, near Glasgow.

And all the time the young Mission was growing. At the end of the third year there were twenty-eight in the work, twelve men and sixteen women. Altogether, eighty-three missions were worked that year, extending in duration from one week to three months. Including these and District work about 1,800 open-air and 3,500 inside meetings were conducted. The total attendance at the latter was 380,000. For a group of unknown and inexperienced young people, to do that in one year was a remarkable feat.

By the end of the fourth year there were thirty-four in the work, fourteen men and twenty women. By the end of the sixth, thirty-seven, and by the end of the ninth year, forty-five. The eleventh annual report reveals that there were forty-six pilgrims who worked 109 missions during the year. Six of these pilgrims were Gaelic-speaking and were working in the Highlands. Forty-six of the 109 missions were held in Ireland. The Mission had crossed the Irish Sea and a number of Irish pilgrims were operating in the Emerald Isle. In fact at the turn of the century, of the sixty-six pilgrims, forty were Scots, twenty were Irish and six were English. That year (1900) 190 missions were conducted and a total of 7,160 meetings were held. The numbers professing conversion showed a considerable increase over the previous year. The work at this stage was equally divided between Scotland and Ireland. Throughout 1901 there was again an increase of meetings with yet a much larger number professing conversion. Although there were only sixty-two pilgrims, the whole work showed a most gratifying improvement.

The accomplishment of this work of course cost money. Pilgrims travel much, they require food and lodging, and rent for halls is quite considerable. 'We have to thank many generous friends for their kind donations, and praise the Lord for the continual supply of all our needs throughout the year', wrote the Chief at the close of the third year. 'The total cost to the Mission for the support of the pilgrims has this year come to £544 4s. 7d., from which we calculate that the cost of each pilgrim for the year has been about £25 0s. 0d.' Yet the young people kept offering themselves for service. Ah! They had caught a glimpse of the glory of another world and were willing to deny themselves so that others might hear the gospel and live. Men and women were lost and they needed a Saviour. The pilgrims had the message, and, cost what it may, that message must be proclaimed.

The first twenty years saw the establishment of a work insignificant in its beginnings, its organization, its possessions, its social status, its influential backing, its financial strength. All that the workers had was God, and in His Power they surged forward from strength to strength.

CHAPTER 7

Triumphs in Scotland and England

Jonathan Edwards declared, 'It has been found by experience, that the tidings of remarkable effects of the power and grace of God in any place, tend greatly to awaken and engage the minds of persons in other places'. Numerous reports of great blessings reached the Faith Mission Headquarters, a few of which found their way into the pages of *Bright Words*. How arresting they are! How remarkable that young people without theological training could go into one community after another and see the mighty hand of God in operation. How awesome that villages could be held in the grip of God, as the pilgrims preached on week after week. Their reports stir and challenge all who read them to pray all the more fervently that God would do it again.

At the close of 1890 the pilgrims found themselves in the centre of a revival at *Whitburn*. A hall holding 600 people was crowded nightly with up to forty being counselled for salvation on many nights. At the close of the first week almost a hundred converts were marching the streets singing heartily the praises of God.

The same year at *Stonehouse* God worked mightily in the seven-week mission, and they saw blessing, 'such as they have not had since 1859'. A Prayer Union with 170 members was formed.

In January 1891 *Cullipool* saw the hand of God in operation. At one meeting when thrilling and spontaneous testimonies poured from the lips of over twenty young men recently converted, the godless exclaimed, 'We have never seen anything like this before'.

In 1897 the impact of the open-air campaign on the town

was so great that the *Oban Telegraph* gave it a most sympathetic review, commenting in amazement at the power of the gospel to transform so many different characters. The soldier, the seaman, the working man, the church-goer gladly told what Christ meant to them and boldly took their stand in the open-air meetings.

In 1900 the president of the YMCA at *Dingwall* reported that the mission conducted by two men 'began quietly until by the end of seven weeks, the hall was packed to its utmost capacity. Such holy joy, boldness and unity of Spirit characterize the converts, and prayer is a marked feature of their lives'.

In 1901 *Fort William* saw a remarkable move of the Spirit when two ladies battled at first against coldness, indifference and prejudice. It was not until the third week that a rift appeared in the clouds, and the soul-saving and sanctifying work commenced. Night after night the hall was filled to overflowing until the Masonic Hall was engaged. Still the numbers increased and still men and women were finding peace with God. The meetings then moved to the Town Hall and on Sunday evenings this too proved too small. Christians were refreshed in the half-nights of prayer. For fourteen weeks it continued with many, many people trusting God for salvation. 'It has been a long time since Fort William has had such a visitation', said a grateful writer. Months later, and still very grateful, the reporter says, 'The work of revival in Fort William during the past winter, has proved solid and substantial'.

Two sisters had a remarkable mission at *Tarbert on Loch Fyne* in 1901, and part of a report which appeared in *Bright Words* reads as follows:

'For the first few weeks it seemed as though the devil was going to have the victory, as there was so much coldness in many of us, God's children, and a fearful indifference in the unsaved . . . In the third week of the mission the Lord brought us to wait on Him in earnest believing prayer for an outpouring of the Holy Spirit . . . In the fourth week the Lord gave us the joy of seeing the first young convert taking his stand for Jesus, who since then has continually been adding souls to our number.

'This has been a special time of refreshing from the presence of the Lord. There has not been for many years past such evidence of the work and power of the Spirit of God, nor a mission held for such a length of time that has been so largely attended. The interest never flagged. During the eleven weeks God has revived the hearts of His own children in a special way . . . and a great number of the unsaved have been brought into saving and living touch with Jesus.'

That was eighty-four years ago. There is no one in Tarbert today who has any recollection of that mission which evidently caused a real stir, nevertheless the fruits of it have reached to the ends of the earth as the following contacts show. Almost thirty years afterwards a minister of the United Church of Canada, a Doctor of Divinity, invited two pilgrims now working in the Dominion, to hold a week of meetings in his church – a large church some sixty miles from Toronto. In the course of these meetings he told the people that he had been saved through the pilgrims at Tarbert in Scotland some thirty years ago, further adding that he knew definitely that there were eight converts of that particular mission in the Christian ministry.

The same year two young ladies went to *Stewarton* and began with very difficult meetings. After special times of prayer with some of the Christians, God began to work and they had to move to a bigger hall. Many trusted Christ for salvation, and after a week of Christian's meetings at the close of the gospel campaign, sixty joined the newly-formed Prayer Union.

At *Aberfeldy* a seven-week mission was extremely fruitful, and at the last meeting 'a great number testified to receiving eternal life during the mission'. A follow-up mission held later saw 'intense interest and much blessing when lasting impressions were made'.

The nine weeks at *Ballachulish* closed with great blessing. Many came to Christ, and 'the Christians' lives were transformed'. The dedicated lives of the pilgrims spoke volumes, and their preaching and singing caused many to take a step of faith.

On the *Isle of Eigg* it was quite a new thing to have pilgrims, and throughout the six-week mission 'they worked with untiring zeal and great faithfulness. Those earnest addresses and heart-stirring appeals we will never forget! Oh, it was glorious as night after night sinners repented of their sins!'

From *Kirriemuir* the minister reports that the church hall soon became too small for the crowds attending the mission conducted by two ladies, and the church had to be used. About 250 attended during the week while on Sunday evenings the church could hardly hold them all. 'It was a time of blessing such as has not been seen here for many years.'

At a *Musselburgh* Prayer Union Rejoining over 100 were present when Mr Pottie spoke on prayer, and before he concluded, 'the spirit of prayer took such a hold upon the congregation that one after another, and sometimes two at a time, were crying to God in tears, for deliverance and for victory.'

Two pilgrims ministered for two months at *West Linton*, 'and many found the Saviour. Christians have entered into the fullness of blessing and have really been set free to serve God. The visit of the pilgrims is a direct answer to prayer and we have experienced 'seasons of refreshing' in this place. To God be the praise and glory!'

At *Cockenzie*, after the third week of a six-week mission, there was scarcely a night on which numbers did not respond to the Gospel appeal. One mother, on being asked if she knew a difference in her home said it was 'like heaven below', and no wonder, for nearly all the members of that family had been converted. Almost a year later a local Christian leader said, 'Nearly every one who came out for Christ when the pilgrims were here, are involved in Christian activities today'.

At *Haltwhistle*, Cumberland, the 'untiring energy and pure devotion of the workers was amply rewarded, and in the six-week campaign over forty professed conversion.

At *Newbattle*, Co Durham, in two weeks of meetings, when the church was filled nightly, over sixty came to Christ and Christians received new vision and mighty blessing.

At *Langholm* from the third week to the end of the seventh week when the mission closed, 'people wept their way to the Cross every night'. The several half-nights of prayer were greatly blessed. 'For the last thirteen years nothing like this has been seen in our town'.

In *Lumley*, after an address by Miss Livingstone one evening, fourteen trusted Christ for salvation. That evening service went on till two in the morning. In the brief two-week mission there were over 100 converts. 'Would that the pilgrims could have stayed longer.'

In *Penshaw* during the fortnight's mission there were about sixty converts, 'and from every point of view it has been the best mission this Methodist Church has had in the history of any of its present members. We cannot speak too highly of the untiring labours of the pilgrims.'

New Herrington saw a 'visitation of divine power and grace' during the visit of two ladies. In this 'magnificent work' over 100 came to Christ, and many Christians made a full consecration to Christ. Some weeks later the minister wrote, 'The mission has proved abundantly fruitful, and we have a large number with us today as a result of the work done, while some have joined other churches. All the places visited nearby were deeply stirred, and a widespread influence exercised for miles around. It is the most remarkable mission ever to be held in the history of this circuit, and will never be forgotten by those privileged to share in it. The sisters are spoken of with the greatest respect by large numbers today.

We give grateful thanks to God for making them a blessing to hundreds of people.'

At *Carlisle* the three-week mission conducted by two ladies was 'the best we have experienced for years'. The meetings were well attended and the Sunday evenings were packed with between 600 and 700. 'Many have come to Christ and we look back on the mission with gratitude to Almighty God!'

What could we more say of so many places missioned? Words expressing wonder and gratitude punctuate the numerous reports of these wonderful days. 'Jesus has been in our midst', 'to God be all the praise and glory', 'at last the answer has come', 'great joy', 'abundant blessing', 'the very atmosphere was charged with the power of the Holy Spirit', 'tears flowed copiously', 'this mighty blessing', 'God has been exalted', 'hallelujah!' – and so we could go on. Report after blessed report could be filed. Thrilling stories of lives, and indeed communities which were completely transformed could be told. In awe we can but exclaim, 'Lord, do it again'.

CHAPTER 8

Stirring Times in Ireland

In the summer of 1891 the Chief was invited to speak at a Conference of the International Police Association in Belfast, where he made the acquaintance of three ladies from Blackrock near Dublin, the Misses May, Emma and Helena Garratt, which began a friendship which was to mean much for the Kingdom in the years that lay ahead.

The Misses Garratt asked the Chief for a pair of pilgrims to conduct a mission at their home in Blackrock, called 'Glenvar'. Horace Govan and Leonard Corsie crossed over, but instead of four days they spent four weeks there with much blessing. At the closing meeting over forty testified and a Prayer Union was formed. Missions followed at Kingstown, Clara, Moate and elsewhere, James Middlemiss taking Horace Govan's place when the latter had to return to Scotland, who commented later in *Bright Words:* 'Will you pray that the results of the Blackrock and Kingstown missions may be felt throughout all Ireland, and that a band of Irish pilgrims may be raised up?' Since those words were written ninety-three years ago, we can see how wonderfully this request has been answered.

Then a call came from Carnlough in Co Antrim, to which place Pilgrims Todd and Middlemiss were sent, and at the close of the mission a Prayer Union was formed. Glenarm was the next opening, and then followed a mission at Cushendall held by Miss Emma Garratt and Pilgrim Hay, where a Prayer Union was also formed. Miss Garratt had to return to Dublin, Miss Hay being joined by other pilgrims who came over from Scotland. One place after another opened up for missions, which were held in many villages and rural districts in Co

Antrim, with Prayer Unions being formed, some of which exist to this day. In December 1892, John George Govan wrote of the Faith Mission work in Ireland, 'What the outcome will be we will not venture to prophesy!' By 1894 the work was firmly established and on 12th of July 1895, conferences were held in a tent at Ballymena which was packed with more than 1,500 people present.

In 1895 the three Garratt sisters were asked to speak at a Methodist Church when on holiday at Killybegs, Co Donegal. This began their great ministry in *Donegal*. These dignified, spiritually-gifted women were welcomed by all classes of the community. Rectors, Methodist and Presbyterian ministers all showed sympathy in meetings at which they spoke, and missions which they held. They exchanged their beautiful home for the simplicities, privations and raptures of pilgrim life, enduring all kinds of rough living in many far-off places where very few of even the normal facilities existed, and they saw a mighty flood-tide of blessing. A newspaper report reads: 'Not since 1859, that memorable year when such a mighty tidal wave of blessing swept over the north portion of our island, have God's people enjoyed such a blessed time as we are at present enjoying in the North-Western district of Donegal'. Another magazine reports: 'During the last three years the Misses Garratt have been working on independent lines, but in connection with the Faith Mission in the surrounding districts of Ballynetherland, Aughinique, Killybegs, Inver, Mountcharles and Ardara and also Donegal. Through their instrumentality hundreds have become participants of God's saving grace.' The hand of God was upon their lives, and even today their names are honoured in Donegal. Some time later when Mr Corsie visited parts of Donegal, he said, 'I had read of the great revival at *Inver*, when Miss H. Garratt was the honoured instrument two years ago; but it was only through visiting and coming into personal contact with the people that one could form any adequate idea of the extent and thoroughness of the work. In some cases whole families had been brought to Christ. Truly the work has been of God, deep and permanent, and much fruit remains to His praise and glory'.

Missions were being held in many places as the pilgrims surged forward. In *Rasharkin*, Co Antrim, the hall was well filled every night; but on Sunday nights the people could not be accommodated. One of the people seated his workshop and a good part of his yard to make room for the numbers which attended. After a half-night of prayer God began to work and during the eight weeks 'a great number' were brought to a saving knowledge of Jesus Christ. Many Christians entered by faith into the full blessing of Pentecost. A strong and vibrant Prayer Union was formed.

Ballymena was the scene of a great movement of the Spirit in 1900. At first the meetings were small with a most unresponsive spirit, but slowly interest increased. One Friday night about seventy Christians met for a half-night of prayer, and this night was the turning point in the campaign. God descended on that praying company in a way which they had never known before. At midnight they were on their knees in great brokenness of spirit crying to God for cleansing and deliverance from every form of inward sin and selfish carnality. Step by step the Holy Spirit led them into the clear light and glorious liberty of God as they claimed the power of the cleansing blood of Jesus and trusted God to fill them to overflowing with the blessed Holy Spirit. Their hearts were filled and their mouths were opened in praise to God for this mighty encounter. It was a never-to-be forgotten night and they would never be the same again. When they reached their homes at two in the morning, they knew that victory was assured.

On the next night the open-air meeting was a rousing time, and the people of Ballymena were stirred. The march assumed the dimensions of some political demonstration, and at the close of a bright testimony meeting, the Holy Spirit fell on the gathering. Twenty people came boldly forward in public acknowledgement of their intention to leave their old ways and turn to Christ for salvation. The following Sunday evening found the hall crowded with the Spirit bringing conviction of sin in mighty power. Numbers responded once again to God's call for salvation. By this time the open-air meetings were attracting large crowds, and the YMCA hall proved too small to hold the people. At the after-meetings many turned to Christ and were soundly converted.

The meetings moved to the Protestant Hall which seats over 1,000, and still there was not room as Brother Hill preached with the anointing of the Holy Spirit upon him. Scores of people kept coming to Christ and trusting Him for salvation.

Another half-night of prayer was held and about eighty crowded in. Mr Pottie denounced half-hearted Christianity and was inspired in testimony. Another mighty time of prayer followed, with confessions and brokenness mingling with prayers, testimonies, and praise. 'Such a time we have never seen', was the comment. 'The reality of eternity and of the presence of God could never be adequately described. Christ was real. The results of that night must travel on into eternity.' Scarcely a night passed without people streaming out to meet with God. Hundreds were unable to gain admission on the last three Sundays. What a time of divine visitation!

At *Kesh* the next year two ladies conducted a six-week mission with splendid results. Night after night the hall was filled, and after the second week there were conversions every night throughout the campaign. At *Ederney* and *Lack*, both in Co Fermanagh, many, many people came to Christ and many a feeble Christian was stirred and brought to a place of full surrender in these life-transforming meetings. The weekly church prayer meetings increased to ten times their previous numbers. The change in the community was dramatic. At *Killagan* in 1902 the mission was held in a barn and for four weeks there was no response. It was on a wet night with a small meeting that the break came when four folk came to Christ. After that the blessings flowed and almost every night people were marvellously converted. 'The secret of the mission's success was believing, prevailing prayer!' said a Christian leader. At the final testimony meeting God was greatly glorified as many rose to tell of what God had done. In fact at times two were testifying at once! One man spoke of having walked 900 miles in six months to attend Faith Mission meetings, for in that time he had attended fifteen campaigns!

At *Ballymarlow* the pilgrims struggled through the first three weeks of hard, unresponsive meetings. People sat unmoved and Christians seemed cold and apathetic. But prayer . . . but God! Soon the heaviness was replaced by an outpouring of the Spirit of God and 'many, very many' turned to Christ as their Saviour. As the news spread through the district, the meetings grew until 'the attendances were the greatest ever seen at any meetings in the district'. A Prayer Union of sixty members was formed. At *Ballyhill*, Co Antrim, the same pattern emerged, and for the first three weeks a fierce battle raged. After that, however, for a further nine weeks, people simply flocked to the Saviour. Tears flowed as many repented and found forgiveness in Christ. On an average there were 250 during the week and 400 on the Sundays. A large Prayer Union was formed at the close of the Mission, which continues to this day.

'We never had a mission here in which a better spirit prevailed, and the two sisters have been mightily used', was the comment on the mission at *Loanends* where an average of 300 attended the weeknight meetings and where 500 streamed in on Sunday evenings. *Dunadry*, Co Antrim, was the scene of a great battle, and for four weeks, despite good congregations, there was no break in the hard, resistant atmosphere. Two half-nights of prayer were held, and during the fifth week thirty adults and thirty children trusted Christ for salvation. From then on interest increased. The atmos- phere was such that the very singing of the hymns brought tremendous conviction of sin. Throughout the rest of this nine-week mission people came to Christ in a continuous stream. During the last week 300 attended the weeknight meetings and 800 came to the final Sunday gathering. 'The public houses rue the day that the tent was erected, for they have lost an enormous amount of business!'

In 1904 two ladies, Robinson and Halliday, conducted a mission which lasted thirteen weeks at *Crossgar*, Co Down, and in the middle of the second week the work of conversion began. The night which stands out is that of the 13th September, almost a month after the mission began. 'The mere mention of the "13th" brings a glow to the faces of many who were born again that night.' The after-meeting was a never-to-be-forgotten experience! There were too many people in the hall for those who were anxious about their spiritual condition to come to the front, so the men and the lads found kneeling space along one end of the hall, row upon row behind each other. The ladies and girls found room at the other end of the hall, while the last to come just surrounded the platform. The power of God was mightily evident. The meeting was in the grip of the Eternal. Hearts were broken and tears flowed copiously as many wept their way to the Cross. The sobs, the cries, the praises all mingled together in heavenly symphony. 'God healed their broken hearts – it was beautiful. What a night!' After this the work went on steadily until the people who remembered the '59 Revival reckoned that there were more conversions in this part of the district at this time than there had been then. Some walked miles to the meetings. One very old man came to the hall just to sit and look at the changed faces of the people he had known so long, and said, 'Thank God! If I can't hear, I can see!'

The fearless, loving concern that the young converts had for others was wonderful. They prayed in the prayer meetings, they spoke to their associates and led them to Christ. One of them (a '13th') writes, 'There have been conversions every night and God is working through those who have decided. It is wonderful to see those who were saved in the early part of the mission sitting with their arms around their companions, leading them to Jesus. It's the way of the young to be hungry, and many crowd in to the converts' meetings and to the prayer meetings.' The pilgrims went on to the next mission leaving hundreds of young Christians supported by the more experienced, growing from strength to strength.

In the Crossgar mission George Gibson was one of the converts, who in the years that lay ahead was destined to be widely known throughout Northern Ireland, as a cattle dealer who was not ashamed to bear witness for his Saviour in markets and fairs, holding open-air meetings as occasions arose. He was greatly respected for his fearless stand for the Lord and for his faithful and consistent witness.

In the same year the Spirit of God worked powerfully at *Stranorlar*, Co Donegal, at an eight-week mission, where from the very first night the conviction of God gripped the people. So many different characters were reached. Wild, reckless men were soundly converted as well as those who lived blameless and upright lives, but whose religion was merely a matter of form without substance or reality.

At *Leitrum*, Co Down, during a 'very blessed nine weeks' mission' the two ladies led about forty to Christ. At *Tullygarley*, Co Antrim, many were led to Christ, and, in this area where there had been no meetings, two weekly services were established, a Prayer Union and a weekly Gospel service. At *Moyroe*, 'Oh, the joy of harvest! One by one they have come and given themselves to God! At *Sandymount*, Co Armagh, people came from apparently nowhere to an eight-week mission held in a barn which held 250 people on the Sunday evenings and over eighty professed salvation. At *Kilkinamurry*, Co Down, two ladies held a seven weeks' mission in a barn. 'We have not seen such a time of blessing since the '59 Revival', ran the report. At *Reilly's Trench*, Co Down, on the first Sunday night three people came to Christ, and from then on 'men and women were born again almost every night. It has been the day of God's power.' At *Drummuck*, Co Antrim, in 1905, 400 gathered at the close of a seven-week mission, which was 'a foretaste of heaven when many, many found the Saviour'. At *Clonatrace*, Co Antrim, in 1906, large crowds gathered for a five-week mission in spite of the extremely cold and boisterous weather. Thirty adults and numbers of children came to Christ. In several cases whole families were simply transformed.

Many more stories could be told, and those that are recorded could be amplified, but these reports give just a little glimpse of some of the victories of those early days. The young pilgrims were filled with a burning desire to see men and women come to Christ, and, inspired and filled with the Holy Spirit, they went out as flames of fire to accomplish mighty victories in the all-powerful Name of Jesus Christ.

God was setting His seal on this advance into Ireland in a remarkable way, and friends were raised up for the Mission, who were destined to be faithful supporters of the work in future years.

Reference has already been made to J. B. McLean, the young gamekeeper, who was led to the Lord at Drymen, the first mission held by sister pilgrims. In a written testimony he refers to himself as the first convert of the mission. In 1890 he joined the band of pilgrims, and after service in Scotland, latterly at the headquarters in Rothesay, he was appointed to take over the leadership of the work in Ireland. He and his wife, a convert of the Rothesay revival, accordingly came to Northern Ireland in 1902. To J. B. McLean the work in Ireland owes an inestimable debt. Under his wise and spiritual leadership the work grew and developed as the years passed. He was an excellent organizer, winning the confidence and respect of the Christian public and the leaders of the religious denominations in Ulster.

CHAPTER 9

Reorganization

After years of strenuous service and heavy responsibility, the Chief found it advisable, and in the Lord's will to be relieved of the leadership of the work for a period. This was approved and in February 1906, his brother Mr Horace Govan, who was editing *Bright Words*, undertook 'the duties of Acting Director'.

The Chief and his family settled in Southport. He had many friends in Southern Africa, and he and his wife responded to an invitation to go there in 1909. They enjoyed almost a year of happy association with Christian folk there, speaking at many mission stations and conferences, not the least with Dr Andrew Murray at his Wellington Convention in the Cape.

Here in Britain the spirit of revival which had been so evident in the first years of the work, and which had burst forth in refreshing streams on so many occasions during the last twenty years, seemed to be receding. This did not apply only to the work of The Faith Mission but was evident throughout the country. Christian activity did not thrive as easily nor develop as quickly. People did not respond as before, and generally the evangelistic scene was more difficult than it had been in 1886. It was not as attractive to endure hardness for Jesus' sake, for the battle was fierce and the cost was great. The number of pilgrims began to decrease in the succeeding years.

The general work of the Mission had reached the stage where reorganization and a sharing of responsibilities were of the utmost importance. The Council meetings at Portrush in August 1911 were crucial. The Chief returned and was appointed President and Treasurer, with Mr Horace Govan continuing as editor of *Bright Words*. The District Superintendents in the three districts were given more authority and a governing council was formed. As these measures were implemented new life seemed to breathe into the Mission. The Chief had that power to kindle enthusiasm and inspire self-sacrificing effort for the salvation of men and women, and his leadership was God's gift to the work just when it was most needed.

In 1905 the great Welsh revival had taken place and expectations for a similar work elsewhere ran high. In many of the missions held by the workers, God blessed in a remarkable way. In a campaign held in the Baptist Church in *Ratho*, Midlothian, over 100 professed salvation, the large majority being young men. At *Clunie*, Perthshire they exclaimed joyfully, 'At last God has come. There has not been a time of such an awakening and blessing for many years'. In *Tranent*, at a six-week mission, thirty-two were soundly converted. From *Elphinstone*, in the Lothians, came the news, 'It was the best mission we have ever had'.

In North Cumberland two ladies had a mission at *Heathersgill*, and 'a great blessing fell on the people'. They moved to *Scaleby Hill* four miles away, and here numbers who had attended the previous mission committed their lives to Christ. 'We have not seen such meetings for forty years. The whole district has been awakened, and revival hymns have almost everywhere taken the place of the usual popular songs.'

In Ireland reports of the Spirit's moving in great power were arriving at the office. In *Ballybeg*, the blessing was such that Christians said, 'This past month has been the best in all our experience'.

In *Kiltinney*, Co Londonderry, numbers from all classes and ages of the community came to Christ. 'We have been the grateful recipients of a gracious outpouring of the Holy Spirit', they said.

Throughout the whole work something happened. A new hope for the future thrilled the hearts and lit the faces.

Somehow the Spirit surged through all parts of the work. Donations and contributions to the work increased and needs were met at the headquarters and on the field. At the close of 1913 there were forty-seven pilgrims in the work, and during 1914 although three resigned, twenty-two joined!

'This year has been our best', writes the superintendent of the South Scottish District. From Ireland came the news that there were 200 more Gospel meetings in 1914 than the previous year, and an increased attendance throughout the year of 20,000. 'Many, many more have been saved than last year.'

A Christian farmer from the border counties of Scotland who knew the Mission, moved to East Anglia. He was burdened with his new countryside and invited the pilgrims to hold missions there. Four sister pilgrims conducted missions in fourteen Suffolk villages in one year. Many were brought to Christ, six Prayer Unions were formed and this new region rapidly developed as a permanent part of the Mission's area of operation.

Saturday conferences all over showed a marked increase in number and in attendance, and were characterized very often by a great sense of the presence of God. In Edinburgh, for instance, 500 were present at the New Year Conference. Of the Dumfries Conference the Chief said, 'The largest conference I have seen here with a very good spirit'. From the North of Scotland came the news, 'A good many pulpits have been opened to the pilgrims all over this part of the country'.

In 1915 Faith Mission work began in South Wales in and around the Gower Peninsula. All parts of the Mission showed advance despite the difficulties associated with the war. In fact, in the North Scottish District alone that year fifty-seven missions were held, and although there was no great revival, 585 people professed conversion.

The first Easter Convention was held at Bangor, N Ireland, in 1916, and because of the war, the second was held in 1919. Thereafter it became an annual event and has had an enormous effect upon the whole of Ireland, gathering together so many who have been blessed through the pilgrims in the country districts, and uniting them in great rejoicing congregations. Men of God from Britain and from other places in the world have ministered in the large packed churches in this, one of the foremost conventions in the British Isles.

Throughout the work, every now and again, there would be a breaking through of God in revival power. In a mission at *Sanquhar* in the South Scottish District, eighty-six professed salvation. At *Carrowcolman*, Co Tyrone, a wonderful time of revival was experienced. On the very first night a backslider was restored and two ladies converted. At nearly every meeting there were conversions, and in many families as many as three or four. A good number trusted God for the fulness of the Spirit. At the children's meetings many came to Christ. 'We have not experienced such a work of grace, no, not since the Ulster revival of '59.'

From Co Armagh comes another stirring report from a Christian leader, 'During the past sixteen months *Annagh-more* and the surrounding districts have been scenes of a great revival such as has not been seen for fifty years. Two sister pilgrims were greatly used by God. Many people have been saved and God's own people stirred as never before. One night when Miss Robertson spoke of "Robbing God", many were melted to tears under the power of God's Word. They will never forget that night! The success of the mission I attribute to three causes: the time spent in prayer; the preaching of sanctification; the fact that the Faith Mission does not form a sect. The churches have been greatly revived'.

From the isolated parts of *Ardnamurchan* in the Western Highlands, comes the news: 'During the last three months Kilchoan and Sanna districts have been the scenes of great revival, such as we have not witnessed for twenty-five years. Two pilgrim brothers, D. Campbell and G. Dunlop, were powerfully used as the instruments of God in the conviction and salvation of souls. Great success has attended this work and the churches have been greatly revived'. (Duncan Campbell later became the Principal of the Faith Mission Bible College.)

A move of the Spirit took place among the Stirlingshire miners in *Blackbraes* near Falkirk. The only services held in the village were those for children – a Sunday School. All attempts to evangelize the village seemed to have failed. Two miners prayed fervently for the place and applied to the Faith Mission for workers. Two ladies came, and from the very outset everyone sensed the presence of God and the power of the Spirit. The numbers increased steadily until 300 gathered in the hall every night. In all, forty adults and over 100 children came to the Saviour. A Methodist minister testified that, 'Great and blessed results have crowned the efforts of the pilgrims'.

At *Kilross*, Co Donegal, the meetings were held in a barn where many found the Saviour. A Prayer Union with thirty members was formed. Great times of blessing were experienced at *Roughan*, Co Armagh, where a Prayer Union was formed with forty members.

At *Falkirk*, Scotland, from the beginning God worked, and hundreds attended nightly. The pilgrims were stopped in the streets and asked the way of salvation, and scores found the Saviour.

The Faith Mission was born in the fires of revival, it had known revival down the years, and nothing would satisfy the pilgrims but a fresh outpouring of the Holy Spirit. They were spoiled for everything else. Entertainment on the Christian scene left them cold. If people must be entertained in the meetings, they are being attracted by means other than by the anointed preaching of the Word of God. Entertainment was seen to be an expression of defeat. God must come, God must save, God must draw, God must conquer. They could rejoice about a meeting only if God moved onto the scene and if folk had glimpses of eternity. Oh for more of the Spirit of God breathing through the activities of men!

At the close of 1921, the Chief said, 'It has been a good year, a very good year. This thirty-fifth year has surpassed any year in the last twenty or more years in the Mission's history. The summer campaign in Oban has been quite the best for some years. Conferences have been inspiring, God's presence has been with us'.

In 1921 an article appeared in *Bright Words* entitled, 'Are we on the Eve of Revival?' 'In our own Faith Mission fields', we read, 'there are indications of a widespread movement of the Spirit of God.' The sixty-four workers in the Faith Mission were waiting, hoping, expecting, praying for the revelation of God in revival power.

CHAPTER 10

Overflowing Blessings

Expectancy for revival was in the air. Special prayer meetings were held in many parts, and people prayed earnestly that God would move across the nation. Places as far apart as Dumbarton and Plymouth were being touched by God. Glasgow felt the impact of the divine Presence.

Revival came to the fisher folk from the North East of Scotland when they were in East Anglia as they followed the annual movement of the herring around the British coast. Yarmouth received a divine awakening and numerous thrilling stories could be told of the outpouring, like the one when a company of girls were jaunting down the street on their way to a dance. A young Scot stood in their way and said, 'Look here, don't you dance yourselves into hell; come right away to the meeting'. Six of them came. 'There they knelt in their evening dress weeping, their dancing shoes beside them; and all six were converted that night.'

The fisher folk returned to the North after the herring season in East Anglia, and took the fire with them. Although signs of the quickening were felt in many churches, the revival was almost entirely amongst the fisher people and it burned all down the North-East coast. Jock Troup, a cooper from Wick, was one of the prominent figures in this movement but many of those who were active in Christian work in those parts were caught up in the flow of the Spirit as well. Public houses, cinemas, dance-halls and other attractions were forsaken, and the prayer meetings were crowded.

'Many people want revival but are not willing to pay the price', said the Chief. 'They are not willing to get all their idols overthrown from their hearts, and from their service.

There must be a destruction of idols and iniquity within, if revival is to come to the individual and to the community. The Holy Spirit comes to search our individual hearts. We do not want a superficial revival; we want the real, deep, thorough work of the Holy Spirit. We must be willing to do away with the carnal elements that have crept in in so many quarters. Revival costs, and the idols must go. There must be a purifying and refining before the filling can come. Are we willing for the religious revolution that deep and widespread spiritual revival may bring? Will you allow the Holy Spirit to search your heart today? Will you come to Calvary and trust Christ to cleanse you now?'

While God was moving in North-east Scotland, God was wonderfully using the great Irish evangelist W. P. Nicholson in Ireland. Mr Nicholson with his sturdy stature, his dramatic genius, his power of swaying men's minds was cast in a mould all his own. His terrific severity, his mother-like tenderness, his utter trust in the Word and the Spirit made him a liberating force to vast numbers of Irish people. Thousands upon thousands responded to the call of Christ in his great campaigns in the towns and cities across Northern Ireland. Worldly pleasures were forsaken. Dance-halls closed for lack of interest and cinemas were empty. Communities were morally transformed. The glorious spiritual awakening cleansed one town after another. Sin was dealt with and men were made righteous. And this, all because there was an old-fashioned belief in an old-fashioned Book, resulting in the proclamation of an old-fashioned Gospel, accompanied by old-fashioned Power, causing many to stand in amazement and say, as they glorified God, 'We have never seen anything like this before'.

And what of the Faith Mission work at this time? It too shared in the awakening in many parts. 1922 was a year of blessed service. The pilgrims were among the fisherfolk in the North-east corner of Scotland, and at *Sandhaven* near Fraserburgh, had great times of blessing and reaping. In many parts it was a year of hard plodding work, yet, praise God, one of glorious victories as well. There were between 3,000 and 4,000 hours of visiting done in each of the five districts of the Mission, quite apart from the thousands of meetings. This intense spiritual labour was richly rewarded.

Two pilgrims, Campbell and Dunlop, went to *Kinlochleven* in the Highlands, and from the very first, God was in the midst. When they left several weeks later, another twenty or thirty had been added to the church, several of whom were the grown-up families of the older Christians. How they rejoiced together!

In Co Antrim several missions were greatly blessed. *Oldstone, Dunadry, Diamond* and *Gortnagallon* were missioned one after the other, and at each place numbers turned to the Lord. *Newtonhamilton*, Co Armagh, a town of some 500 people with twenty-seven public houses, was visited by two lady pilgrims. There was tremendous blessing as the large hall, crammed with people, was filled with the presence and power of God. The work amongst the young people was wonderful, with often four or five in a family finding the joy of God's salvation. God stepped into the community gladdening hearts, brightening homes and transforming the lives of many Christians.

Dromore, Co Down, was another scene of conflict and victory. Large numbers streamed to the campaign in the Methodist Church. More than seventy people came to the Saviour. Christians were simply thrilled as one after the other burst through into the joy of God's great salvation. In some cases parents wept for joy as their children came to Christ, and in others, both parents and children saved together in the mission, hugged one another as the tears flowed freely. The happy converts witnessed everywhere with tremendous joy and enthusiasm.

On and on went the pilgrims, from village to village, from home to home, preaching to one or two people across the tea-table, speaking at the doors, meeting people on the roads and challenging them about their standing with God, gathering the children for their special meetings – and then down to prayer. Prayer for the neighbourhood when they wrestled for people to be saved, for God's Kingdom to be extended, for the mighty power of God to be revealed. Then to the meetings they went. They thrilled to the battle; they knew the grim determination of faith, the faint gleam of divine light, the breaking through of divine power, the sobbing of the penitent, the glad cries of delight of the saved and the delivered – ah, is there anything like it in all the world?

'The revival began last year in some parts of the country', ran the 1922 annual Irish report from J. B. McLean, 'and how we longed for it to spread. We have not been disappointed, for, as we look over our statistics, we find that the results of the year just closed are more than double those of last year and far surpass anything we have previously known. Apart from one mission held in Belfast, the work has been altogether in the country districts and in one or two small towns. At no time has the prospect been brighter than now, and we look hopefully forward to greater things this winter'.

And greater things there were, for early in 1923 we read, 'The revival movement which has been growing steadily in Ireland is still moving onward. Faith Mission pilgrims are sharing in the harvest'. Pilgrims found themselves in the revival tide.

Hillsborough, Co Down, was once again visited by pilgrims with wonderful results. At *Corlea*, Co Monaghan, the spirit of indifference was eventually broken and the Gospel once again proved to be 'the power of God unto Salvation'.

At *Jerrettspass*, Co Armagh, the spirit of revival and prayer made it easy for almost 100 folk, both old and young, to surrender to the claims of Christ. 'We never knew a mission where God's mighty presence so swamped methods and workers.'

At *Maralin, Lurgan*, on the shores of Lough Neagh, in Co Donegal, and in many other places, the story is the same:

'God is working', 'mighty times', 'many converts', 'lives transformed', 'the hush of eternity', 'the Holy Spirit fell on the meeting', 'what singing!'

It was during this year that a Faith Mission monthly conference was begun in Belfast on similar lines to that which had been held in Edinburgh for many years. The attendance far surpassed all expectations, and on some occasions during this and the succeeding few years, over 2,000 were present, the great majority being converts of the recent missions.

In Scotland, *Ardnamurchan* was again visited by Duncan Campbell and a fellow pilgrim named Steedman, and the Spirit of God was poured out in yet a more abundant measure than before. 'Many came to Christ, and a Prayer Union was begun with sixty members.'

And what of the great mission at *Balintore*, East Ross-shire? It lasted for seventeen weeks with the two Brothers M'Kie and Young. 'Never did the interest flag; instead each week saw greater numbers attending until many were unable to enter on the Sunday evenings and had to stand outside. The Shekinah glory seemed to fill the place. What indescribable joy it gave to the older Christians as scores of young men and women came under the power of the Gospel and yielded to the Saviour! To be present in the meetings was to breathe the atmosphere of Heaven. It was holy ground. What singing, praying, weeping, rejoicing! One saw the shining faces of the converts, heard their testimonies and joined in the hearty singing. The drunken, the careless, the self-righteous, the scoffer, were all brought into the fold. Dozens walked, cycled and motored from several miles away and the blessing spread. The villages were transformed. The impression made on the life of the district has been incalculable, with the publicans complaining of slackened trade, concerts and dances no longer an attraction, while the church prayer meetings have multiplied their attendances many times, and the general life of the churches has been transformed. The converts never tire of testifying and many times 11 p.m. passed with no desire to go home. Over 230 confessed Christ as Saviour, while several claimed the fulness of the Spirit in sanctifying power. Praise His Name!'

And what shall we say of *Ballyrobin* and *Corby* in Co Antrim, of the campaigns in Suffolk, Norfolk, in the North of England and in Scotland? Only this – God has worked, and to Him be the praise and glory.

There were nearly ninety workers in the Mission this year, and twenty-three students in the Training Home. In Ireland alone during the year, pilgrims spent 7,000 hours visiting, had 2,502 Gospel meetings, 800 meetings for Christians, and 300 youth and children's meetings. In addition many open-air campaigns were held with hundreds of meetings. Says J. B. McLean, 'It has been by far the most fruitful year of all our years of work in Ireland'.

In the Annual Report Mr Govan said, 'And now the Mission has come to the close of its thirty-seventh year, and I think statistics will show it has been one of the most fruitful and successful in its history. We have sought, amid all the necessary extension, to keep to the simplicity, the faith, the love, and the whole-hearted devotion and self-denial our Master called us to in our beginnings. Faith Mission service has never been a money-making or high-salaried affair. The way of the Cross is the path to spiritual blessing that also leads to the salvation of others, and self-sacrifice is a necessary adjunct to successful endeavours to 'lift up the fallen, tell them of Jesus the mighty to save'.

CHAPTER 11

Fruit for their Labour

Revival in the north-east of Scotland; revival in Ireland; touches of it all over, but there was no widespread national movement. Christians everywhere, however, kept praying and expecting God to come sweeping through the country.

The Faith Mission work continued to grow, and people came to Christ in scores of villages each year. In Suffolk the work continued until, in 1925, an English District was formed. At Elmsett, in Suffolk, two pilgrims saw a move of the Spirit when thirty-six came to Christ. 'The place has been revolutionized', ran the report.

Many trophies of grace were gathered in far-off places which would never be imagined as likely scenes of a revival. In one mission seven were saved in one house, 'and it was glorious to hear the father or some of the children call out their favourite chorus in the meetings: "Where everyone loves Jesus, it's a happy, happy home" '. In a scattered district in Co Monaghan an old man said that there had been no conversions there since the '59 revival, 'but, thank God, a dozen people have now been saved'. At *Warrenpoint*, Co Down, we read of 'God's wondrous workings', as numbers of young men dedicated themselves to God's service. In three places, *Bellaghy* and *Tullygarley* in Co Antrim, and *Agivey* in Co Londonderry, over two hundred sought the Saviour, influencing a wide area.

From Scotland came the news that in *Leven*, Fife, there were two months of meetings with a weekly day of prayer attended by between twenty to thirty people. 'Conversions right from the start – of all ages.' In *Tranent* 'a score of converts took their stand in the open air'. In Adelphi Hall,

Paisley thirty were converted: 'Wonderful times, nothing like it for twenty years'; *'John O'Groats* can never be the same again', run the reports. 'Large crowds with a number of married couples coming to Christ together, and particularly numbers of young men, taking their stand for Christ. From the misty *Isle of Skye* comes the news of a movement of the Spirit under the ministry of two pilgrims, one of whom was Duncan Campbell. Two young women on the Island, converts of a previous mission who knew how to pray were greatly burdened for their village, and perhaps their prevailing prayers began it all. One night leaving the meeting, one of them said to the pilgrims, 'God is going to work; souls will be saved, but we must fight the battle on our knees'. During that night God so burdened her that she went to the other girl's home between 12 and 1 o'clock in the morning, and said, 'God has come and we must pray through!' They prayed right on until six in the morning. The next evening the power of God fell upon the meeting. 'You would have heard souls groaning under the mighty power of the convicting Spirit of God', said Campbell. 'One woman left the meeting crying "I am lost! I am lost! There is no mercy for me!" Another woman brought her back, but I could do nothing with her. That woman met with Jesus and was gloriously saved. The work of grace had begun.' Much of the Faith Mission work could not be called revival, but certainly there were some blessed results.

In 1922 a young Cambridge graduate, John Eberstein, who later was to become President of the Mission, entered the Training Home. His pilgrim work started in the *Clogher Valley*, in Northern Ireland, and in the three years of working there he, together with other pilgrims, saw hundreds profess conversion. The first mission in *Ballygawley*, which lasted seven weeks with forty professions of salvation, began the wonderful time of reaping. Night after night the people were saved, until when it did not happen for two nights running, he writes in his diary: 'I wonder what is wrong. I must walk closer to God!' Eight weeks in *Aughnacloy* yielded a harvest of almost 100 souls. Then to *Curlough* they went, to *Lisnaweary, Augher* and to many other villages and rural districts as the way opened. In 1985 he had the joy of attending the annual rejoining of the Prayer Union at Killyfaddy, which he had begun 60 years before. Happily he is still with us, and has made the contribution which follows:

'I shall never forget the joy of those wonderful years spent in the Clogher Valley where so many were led to the Lord. It has been my privilege to pay occasional visits to some of the places where missions were held in those far-off days and to find fruit which remained with the children of those who professed conversion at that time following in their parents' footsteps.

'At the end of the first year a conference was held in Ballygawley, of which a contemporary report tells of a godly Christian farmer who "had six children converted". He was so overcome with joy that he "went away to the top of the hill, and sang praises to God at the top of his voice". All his family married and set up Christian homes, several of the next generation being in full-time Christian service. Three of these became pilgrims in the Faith Mission; one is now a missionary in Nepal, another in Sudan, and the third engaged in work amongst children in the homeland. Another was a medical missionary in Nigeria for some years, and is now a surgeon in a hospital in Northern Ireland.

'In 1975 I attended the Centenary Convention at Keswick and met two grey-haired ladies, whom I did not recognize, but it turned out that as young women in Ballygawley they had come into a vital experience of the Lord Jesus Christ. Their sister, a missionary in India, had recently died and she also had been a convert of that same mission.

'My last mission in the Clogher Valley was near Fivemiletown, in *Dernavogie* Orange Hall (since burned down), at which a small boy attended the meetings. In his testimony for *Life Indeed* some forty years later, he wrote that the seed which was sown then "did not die, but lay dormant in my heart for years", coming later to fruition. The small boy of 1926 was the founder of the well-known Killadeas Convention in Northern Ireland.

'I had planned to return to the Clogher Valley after my annual holiday, but the Lord had other plans. Many had been praying for a long time for openings for the Mission in what was then known as the Irish Free State (now the Republic of Ireland) where apart from Co Donegal, all evangelistic work seemed to have ceased since the "troubles" of the twenties, apart also from the larger cities. Mr J. B. McLean told me, that an opening had been secured in Tramore in Co Waterford, saying that he would like me to go, to which I readily agreed.

'It is interesting to know how prayer was answered for the opening up of the work here. A retired Christian business man in Co Waterford, Mr H. S. Atkins, was deeply concerned about the spiritual need of the South. He heard of the work of the Faith Mission, wrote to Mr McLean and on receiving a favourable reply made arrangements for the mission in *Tramore* in October. It is also an illustration of the perfection of God's timing, for Mr Atkins was taken ill in November and died in February. The opening up of the work in the South was almost the last piece of service he did for the Lord.

'We had no idea where our next mission was to be, but doors wonderfully opened, first of all in *Clonmel* which led to further openings in *Co Tipperary*, and then came *Abbeyleix*, with missions in that area and later in *Wicklow* and *Wexford*. At the Bangor Convention in that year the Chief asked me if I would become Superintendent for the South. Having been almost four years in the Mission, I was uncertain as to what the next move was to be. The word the Lord gave me was: "Thou wilt show me the path of life". That settled the matter for me.'

Mr Eberstein worked in the South of Ireland until being

asked to go to Canada in 1930 to see the work of the Mission established there.

An interesting testimony from these days comes from one who became widely known in evangelical circles. Two pilgrims were holding a mission in *Cork* when a boy of twelve made a profession of which he was to write later in a testimony which appeared in *Bright Words*: 'I was attracted by the singing and the brightness that prevailed in the meetings so I went again and again. There was a sense of reality which possessed me, and one night I responded to an appeal for those who wished to be saved. I remember little of what was said, but I know that I definitely put my trust in Christ and was saved'. On leaving school he went to Trinity College, Dublin, after which he was ordained in the Church of Ireland as a curate in Portrush. The boy in question was the Rev A. W. Rainsbury, who served during the war years as an Army chaplain in the Middle East and in Italy, where his witness was greatly blessed, and many were led to the Lord. After a period as Travelling Secretary in Scotland for the Inter Varsity Fellowship (now the University and Colleges Christian Fellowship) he was appointed Vicar of Emmanuel Church, South Croydon, a centre of evangelical witness for many years. Here he had a most fruitful ministry, as well as in South Africa and other places overseas to which he was invited. He was also one of the speakers at the Keswick Convention. In 1984 he went to be with his Saviour, but he never forgot his debt to the Faith Mission or to the two pilgrims who were the means of leading him to the Lord.

Another testimony comes from someone who is well-known in the academic evangelical world: 'Throughout the late 1920's the pilgrims were active in a number of communities in the county of East Lothian. They had to grapple with the native reticence and reserve of the cautious, taciturn East Lothianers. However, the pilgrims' enthusiasm and cordiality won access to many homes; their forthright, down-to-earth declaration of Christ reached many hearts; the Holy Spirit brought many to repentance and faith; and the converts met regularly for fellowship in the various Prayer Unions which were then inaugurated.

'Then, within these prayer cells a subsequent work of grace was effected, for from the Prayer Unions in East Lothian, and in a village just within Midlothian, seven young men entered the ministry of the Church of Scotland.

'And what occurred in East Lothian has been duplicated times without number throughout the hundred years' history of the Faith Mission. It is an irrefutable fact that through the bond maintained by the Faith Mission with the main-stream denominations many hundreds of young men and women, whom the Faith Mission nurtured in the Bible, and trained in prayer, have answered Christ's call to ministry and mission, at home and overseas.'

The contributor of the above, one of the seven young men referred to as having entered the ministry, was the Rev Dr James G. S. S. Thomson. After his conversion he came to the Faith Mission Training Home (as it was called then) following which he spent a period in the work before going to North Africa as a missionary with the Algiers Mission Band, serving in that field for some years. On his return home he studied for the ministry, graduating with high honours, and was awarded a scholarship to Oxford, where he was elected Casbred prizeman of St John's College. After this he was for some years lecturer in the department of Hebrew and Oriental languages in Edinburgh University, during which time he also lectured at our Bible College. Then followed some years in the USA in the Columbia University. On returning to Scotland he was a parish minister till his retirement. The story of his own conversion follows:

'Two pilgrims came to mission the village of Wallyford, which was not far from the town in which I was reared. My mother persuaded me to attend a meeting during that campaign. The service made little impression on me. Indeed my memory of what took place is remarkably vague. And yet although I was so complacent and unmoved, I realise now that such a simple act as the laying of the pilgrim's hand on my arm, and the query put so shyly and so modestly: "What are you going to do about it all?" was for me the act and the word of the living God, who is always confronting us, always challenging us in the ever-present here and now. On that never-to-be-forgotten night the sluice gates of the soul were burst open, and torrents of saving grace swept over me. I can still recapture vividly the sense of wonder that invaded me on that autumn evening more than fifty years ago. And for me to regain that sense of awe is to enter a holy of holies in my soul, which the ruthless hands of a hostile world have never been able to demolish.'

At the close of 1927 there were 110 in the Mission, a few of whom left the Faith Mission for the mission fields. The Mission was not only being effective in the home country, but it was also a channel, providing the mission fields with workers. Former pilgrims were found in many countries with numbers of missionary societies.

All these years God had cared for the Mission, providing all its needs and revealing Himself as Jehovah-Jireh; so much so that the President could say, 'Without appeals or advertisements for money, without sales of work, collectors or collecting boxes, sufficient supplies from our Heavenly Father have come in, not only to keep the work going, but to increase and extend. What a testimony faith work is to the reality of God, the certainty of His Word, and the assurance that He does hear and answer prayer!'

Faith Mission Conventions were a means of great blessing when Christians gathered in times of warm and hearty fellowship. Rothesay, of course, was the first of these conventions, but others developed as well. There were times of refreshing at the Peebles Convention, at St Andrews, at Bangor, N Ireland. In 1926 two other conventions were begun, Larne and Perth.

CHAPTER 12

The Chief's Homecall and Leadership Changes

It was at the Scottish Convention, held for the second year in succession at Perth in September 1927, that the Chief was to leave his beloved pilgrims and enter into the presence of the King whom he had served so well. He spoke to the pilgrims on the journey of Elijah and Elisha before Elijah was translated, showing the typical significance of the different places, leading on to the moment when Elijah was caught up to Heaven. For him too the chariot of fire was sweeping down, and soon he would be away. At the opening meeting of the Convention he spoke from Isaiah 58: 'Cry aloud, spare not, lift up thy voice like a trumpet, and show my people their transgressions, and the house of Jacob their sins'. 'He spoke with great earnestness, intensity, vision and fire. It seemed all so very prophetic. He was transmitting the commission. He was handing on the flame', remarks Mr Percy Bristow, then a District Superintendent, but later to be Secretary and Treasurer of the Mission and to exert a great influence as a very able, clear-thinking leader.

Before the night was out the stroke had fallen, and after three days of unconsciousness, he passed from this earthly battlefield in the midst of his 'soldiers' whom he inspired to the last, into the presence of the One he loved supremely. The Chief was gone.

At the funeral, Dr Graham Scroggie said, 'There must be a deep joy in the hearts of most of us this afternoon – a joy that God spared His servant for so long in such a service, that He enabled him to make an impression on thousands of hearts, not only in Scotland, but in Ireland, and in England and in other spheres. If our gathering together this afternoon leads up to be better men and women, more considerate of others, more humble and true in our devotion to the Lord's service, then out of death comes life, and out of the loss gain everlasting. If he could whisper one word to us gathered here this afternoon, he would say, "Don't sorrow, sing! Don't drop your hearts in despair because I am no longer able to lead the Mission; carry on! The time is short; the fight is great, and the Master of the House is urgent" '.

On his gravestone in Edinburgh are the words which he so often quoted, 'I love my Master . . . I will not go out free'. (Ex 21:5)

The obvious choice for the leadership of the Mission at this juncture was his brother, the Rev Horace E. Govan, who had been closely associated with the work almost from the beginning. After his university career he had joined the Mission in 1888, having a special love for the work in the Scottish Highlands which was maintained throughout his life. In 1912 he was ordained in the Congregational Church in Scotland, holding three pastorates in succession at Forfar, Ardrossan and Edinburgh (Albany Street), resigning from the latter in 1925 in order to give his whole time to the work of the Mission. He was the youngest member of the Govan family, gracious and scholarly, a gifted writer and poet, and there are several of his hymns in 'Songs of Victory'. He edited *Bright Words*, the Mission's magazine, ever since it was handed over by the Rev C. G. Moore in 1889, as a small half-penny paper.

He was, however, President for only a little over four years, being called into the Lord's presence after a brief illness in April, 1932, to be followed three months later by the Chief's widow, which was a great loss to the whole Mission.

Mr J. A. A. Wallace of Lochryan became the next President. He had been a long-standing friend of the Chief, and had had some share in the work in Fife in the early days in that county. Mr P. S. Bristow became Treasurer, and Mr T.

Belford the Director of the Scottish work. Mrs Horace Govan agreed to carry on her husband's work as Editor but she too passed into the Lord's Presence quite unexpectedly in 1934, when John Eberstein was appointed Editor, a position which he filled with distinction till 1968.

The second world war was over, and it was expected as wartime restrictions were lifted, that more students would apply for training, with more pilgrims therefore available for missions, and that there would therefore be an upsurge of spiritual life and witness. But as far as the Mission was concerned it was recognized that those in positions of leadership were well on in years, and Mr J. B. McLean was anxious to retire after fifty-three years in the Mission and over forty in charge of the work in Ireland. Much thought and prayer was given to this situation after which the statement which follows by the President, Mr J. A. A. Wallace was made in *Bright Words*.

'During the last week in April (1945) the Council met for some most important meetings at which vital decisions were made which will have a far-reaching influence on the future of the work. There has been much prayer beforehand and we believe we have been clearly led as a Council in coming to a decision which is as follows:

1. A retiring age was fixed for workers in the Faith Mission. Mr J. B. McLean had already intimated his intention of retiring, and under this rule Mr J. S. Gillespie and Mr T. Belford will also retire from the active leadership of the Mission, though they will still be Council members, giving advice and help, and they will be ready to assist in any way that they are able.

2. Mr J. G. Eberstein, MA, was appointed Director of the whole Mission, while continuing as Editor of *Bright Words*.

3. Mr P. S. Bristow was appointed General Secretary of the Mission, Treasurer of the Mission's funds and Director of the

work in Scotland, with charge also of the work in the South Scottish District.

4. Mr G. E. M. Govan was appointed Director of the work in Ireland, with charge also of the Central Irish District.'

There were other decisions made also at that time, but we only give here those applying to the leadership of the work.

In 1945 Miss Govan also returned to Scotland after being seven years in South Africa. She was married in November, 1946, to Mr Andrew Stewart of Edinburgh, who died in 1952. Mrs I. R. Govan Stewart was the author of 'Spirit of Revival', the biography of her father and the story of the early years of the Mission, the fourth edition of which was produced in 1978. This book, to quote Dr Graham Scroggie, 'simply throbs with spiritual power and holy emotion'. It has been widely read and greatly blessed. It has introduced the Mission to many who would otherwise not have known of its existence, and many have been called through it into the Lord's service. She was also the author of quite a number of other books, which will continue to speak long after she has gone. Her gifts of personal charm, warm friendliness, the spirit of joy and optimism, her spiritual depth and sensitivity of spirit all combined to make her a most talented and useful member of Christ's Kingdom. She died on October 24, 1983, and her brother, Ellis Govan, passed away seven months previously in Zimbabwe, thus severing the last links with the family of the Chief.

In the January 1947 issue of *Bright Words* John Eberstein wrote: 'Seldom does it fall to the lot of any one organization to suffer a triple bereavement among its leaders within the space of a few days, as has been the experience of our Mission. We deeply regret to announce the Home-going of three valued leaders and comrades, whose passing leaves a tremendous blank for us all, and we know ourselves to be much the poorer for the loss of their counsel, their support and their prayers.

'On November 16, at Kinlochleven, Thomas Belford passed away unexpectedly, after a short but severe illness, having been until recently the Director of the work in Scotland.

'Within four days of his death came the news of the sudden Home-going of the beloved President of the Mission, John Alexander Agnew Wallace at his home at Lochryan.

'On the same day that our President died, one of the two Vice-Presidents of the Mission, Hubert Wingfield Verner, was taken peacefully to his Heavenly Home after a short time of extreme weakness and suffering.

'The loss of three valued Council members at such a time is a very real one, and we can but bow our hearts in the presence of One Who makes no mistakes in the sure knowledge that His Spirit remains among us, and He has His own plans for the furtherance of the work He has called into being, and in this confidence we go forward, each member of the Mission claiming afresh the promises of God and relying on His Power.'

In April the Council appointed John Eberstein to succeed Mr Wallace as President. In 1968 after more than forty-five years in the Mission, he retired from his executive responsibilities at Headquarters, which were taken over by Mr Albert Dale. He, however, remained President till 1981, when he felt he should finally retire, his links with the Mission being maintained as Honorary President. The Mission owes much to this sane, spiritual, meticulously careful leader. At one stage he was seriously ill, and a brain tumour was diagnosed. An operation was successfully performed. The tumour was not malignant as had been feared and he calmly recovered to lead the Mission for a further thirteen years. His editor's pen he laid down as well. His job had been well done.

Inevitable changes in leadership take place at irregular intervals for a variety of reasons, and in 1956 the Chief's younger son Ellis Govan to whom reference has already been made, was released from Belfast for an itinerant ministry, as

Vice-President of the Mission, Mr R. Fraser taking his place as Director of the Irish work. At the same time Mr A. Dale was transferred to Edinburgh, with particular responsibility for the Bookroom and Publishing Department.

In 1958 Mr P. S. Bristow retired after a long and exceedingly useful life in the Mission as a wise and spiritual counsellor, and an able administrator. John Eberstein, the President and Editor of *Bright Words*, took over the duties of Treasurer, and Albert Dale was appointed Director of the work in Scotland and England.

After nine years as Director of the work in Ireland 'Roddy' Fraser was due to retire and Mr William Black was appointed to the Central Irish District and given charge of the Irish work. He was held in high regard in Northern Ireland, and the Mission's leadership in Ireland seemed to be in good hands with Bill Black as leader of the work there. But it was not to be. On August 16, 1967 he was suddenly called home, this spiritual Great-heart for whom all felt such a spontaneous affection. It was certainly a blow to the whole Mission family. Mr E. Fox was later appointed as the leader of the work in Ireland.

The year 1968 has already been referred to with regard to John Eberstein's retiral, and Albert Dale taking over his responsibilities at Headquarters. The work in Yorkshire and the Midlands was most encouraging and Mr David Howden who was located in York was given charge of the work in England, and Mr John Farquhar, who had come over from Ireland, of the work in Scotland.

The Mission was under new leadership yet all the men had worked together for years; they understood each other; they understood their pilgrims and they understood the work. Although there were changes in the leadership therefore, it was to a large degree but a continuation of that which they were already doing in slightly different roles with added responsibilities.

Another inevitable change in positions of leadership

occurred when John Farquhar was suddenly promoted to glory, on 17 January, 1972, after almost thirty years in the Faith Mission. Gracious, quiet, consistent and highly valued, he was sorely missed. Mr W. J. Porter was given the appointment of the leadership of the work in Scotland coming to Edinburgh in July 1974.

For a short time Albert Dale was President of the Mission till his final retiral in 1983. The contribution he has made to the work is incalculable, and in his position as leader he united the work on both sides of the water as possibly no one else could have done. 'I know of no one who has given himself more fully or more sacrifically, with a single eye to the glory of God and the good of the Mission during some forty years of service', was the General Director's comment when he retired.

His place was taken as President, at the invitation of the Council, by the Rev Thomas Shaw, a former pilgrim, who is now a Congregational minister in Northern Ireland, with Mr Keith Percival as General Director, in which capacity he also oversees the work in Scotland, and is Treasurer of the Mission's funds. Mr W. J. Porter is Director for the work in Ireland, and Mr J. McNeilly for that in England. These with the Rev Colin Peckham, the Principal of the Bible College, form a team of relatively young men. Should they be spared in the purposes of God, a fairly stable future seems to lie ahead at the beginning of the Mission's second century. Yet in the warp and woof of life we are surely all in the Hands of God and cannot tell what the next day may bring. The leadership is His. He appoints and enables. He is the Chief Shepherd and Guide and our eyes are upon Him as we set out into the unknown future.

CHAPTER 13

On with the Work!

The year that the Chief died 300 missions were held with more than 4,000 professions of conversion. The eight districts were operating efficiently with eighty-seven workers in 1930. During the six years up to and including 1932, spanning the Presidency of Horace Govan an enormous amount of successful work was done when pilgrims held 1,712 missions, visited for 132,469 hours and recorded 17,700 cases of those who professed salvation.

Of course it is possible to count as having professed conversion those who experience no spiritual change, and similarly there are others who come to a knowledge of Christ whose names are never recorded in any earthly book. To be complete we would have to compute statistics of spiritual prosperity, of edification, of love, of humility, of secret prayer, and of other aspects of life which go to make up the full picture. Nevertheless statistics have their value. They give some indication of the progress of the work from year to year. These figures are recorded, however, as 'six of the hardest years of the Mission's history'! Some hardship!

Yet there were hardships. We read of two missions 'which had no decisions amongst the unconverted, but in one of them a number of Christians were revived'. On the whole it was 'stiff and hard', we read of another place, 'yet what encouraged us most was the work amongst the children'. 'The ground proved hard and unfruitful', was another comment. We read of 'hard fighting, fierce opposition, agonizing in prayer, steadfast endurance'. 'Every mission has seen souls saved', comes the report from the North

71

Irish District, 'but generally people, even when convicted, have been slow to yield'.

During this period, through difficulties and trials, the pilgrims continued tenaciously, often plodding on in areas which yielded little fruit and offered scant encouragement. Said one: 'A crippling spirit of pessimism which too frequently appears in the guise of a friend saying, "I think you would be better to try elsewhere, this place is hopeless", has to be continually resisted; otherwise we might be tempted to ask, "Can God?" But as we call to remembrance His working, we are ready to transpose these words with "God can!" Hallelujah!' Yes He can, throughout British Isles and all the way up to Shetland, which the pilgrims visited with great profit at this time.

Pilgrims had been so used to the movements of the Spirit that when only forty-six people came to Christ in three months in the East Scottish District, the report runs, 'You see with what difficulty souls are won'. In East Anglia too we find that 'missions have been slow recently', but good work was done nevertheless, and at one place during a five-week campaign 'thirty-one people came to Christ'.

Conferences and conventions all over continued to be sources of great encouragement to many. In 1935, 500 attended the 469th Edinburgh Conference. That in itself was an indication of blessing and appreciation. After one conference an honoured minister commented, 'the nearest approach to revival that I have seen anywhere'. Christmas conferences, New Year conferences, Twelfth of July conferences in Ireland, Spring conferences, monthly conferences – the people streamed to these all over the country.

In 1936, the Jubilee Year, forty-four pairs of pilgrims were at work. God greatly blessed their labours in the thousands of meetings held and in the thousands of hours of patient visiting. On the average thirty-five folk came to Christ for salvation every week throughout the year, and thirty-four Prayer Unions were begun. It was a year of blessing, yet behind the victories there lay many hours of hard work, much prayer and many hours of demanding counselling. People, however, were saved all over by the mighty workings of the Holy Spirit.

The first quarter of 1938, we hear, 'has been decidedly a time of reaping. Alike in the Hebrides and East Anglia souls have been saved. Through much hardness the tireless band has pressed on, and here and there it has pleased God to give more than the usual increase'.

One very bright spot in this period was the movement in the Roe Valley, Co Londonderry, Ireland. 'How glad we are', they say, 'to bear witness to such times of blessing, in the salvation of sinners, the restoration of backsliders and the sanctifcation of believers. From the start souls were arrested and enlightened, secret followers made open confession; there was a breath of the Spirit over the neighbourhood. At the next mission, four miles away, the Presbyterian Hall was full and some walked for many miles. As the weeks went on the conviction deepened. People filled the hall; they sat everywhere even around the feet of the pilgrims. Then the break came when several young men made their way to Calvary. Thereafter there was great rejoicing as night after night people were pointed to the Saviour. The mission lasted nine weeks. The third mission just a little farther along also lasted nine weeks, and several convicted at the previous one, came to Christ, while others sought heart-cleansing and the fullness of God's Spirit. Disheartened Christians were encouraged, backsliders restored, careless souls convicted and converted. Families were united in Christ. Restitution was made. Sabbath-breakers now attend a place of worship. Tobacco and cards were destroyed. Two busloads of these people who have been so blessed went to the last Ballymena Conference. What great joy! What a spirit of gladness and glory in this great work of grace. Hallelujah!'

It was in the Roe Valley in June 1938 that a young business man, Albert Dale, whose contribution to the leadership of the Mission in coming years was to be very great, was converted under the ministry of one of the lady pilgrims. In the purposes of God what vital contacts are made sometimes in the least unexpected moments. The pilgrims never knew what the eventual outcome of a mission would be as they led one and another to Christ, but they pressed on in the assurance that God would establish and guide those who placed their trust in Him.

Although there were some very hard missions in 1938 it was a fruitful year, with one-third more folk seeking salvation in the 299 missions than in either of the two previous years. In East Anglia we read of 'many outstanding cases of conversion'. A mission in Ayrshire yielded a harvest of 'forty bright new Christians'.

In the Western Isles there seemed to be very definite quickening. Meetings were blessed with some of the converts 'walking up to twenty miles to meetings, singing along the roads as they came'. Some of the meetings were difficult to close and went on to midnight, and beyond! Full of the Lord's presence they were, with the people hungry for the Word and happy in the Lord. A refreshing breeze was blowing across the Island of Lewis cheering the hearts of the Island folk. The District Superintendent says, 'Full halls, good spirit, bright converts. Never had so much liberty in my soul'.

A pilgrim's life is certainly far removed from monotony, and in the interests of the Kingdom the experiences which they endure or enjoy are sometimes quite memorable. As they crossed from one island to another in a small boat a pilgrim reported, 'My fellow-worker thought that we were going to a watery grave and was tempted to envy me because I lay helplessly sick at the bottom of the boat and did not see the stormy waves'.

'We crossed the fords at low tide', said another sister pilgrim, 'wading through the icy water which was up to and above our knees. On the other side we dried as best we could and then set off to visit the scattered homes in the community'.

'What a thrill after walking the two miles to the little hall every night', said another, 'to see the lanterns and lamps coming over the hills in the darkness. They came from all over and converged on the hall. It was cold, so the men strung a wire at the back of the hall and hung up their lamps giving us such cosy warm meetings'.

Sometimes meeting places would be quite unconventional. A barn could be cleaned, scrubbed and sometimes given a coat of emulsion as well to make it acceptable and attractive. The inventive genius of the pilgrims knew no bounds.

Many miracles of God's marvellous provision could be told. 'Our provisions had come to an end', said one. ' "Oh Lord", I prayed at the table, "please send us a loaf of bread", and before I could say "Amen", there was a knock at the door. There stood a boy with a newly-baked loaf of bread. "My mother sent me with this for you", he said simply.' That young pilgrim went on in the service of God to trust Him for many thousands of pounds, but the faith principle was being taught right at the beginning. How precious was that loaf of bread!

In the realm of finance, the exact amount has come to meet a specific need on many occasions. With such a tender touch our loving Heavenly Father sees to so many tiny details. Little 'coincidences' of Divine favour cause humility and deep gratitude to well up in the pilgrim's heart to the God who saw the needs even before they were expressed in prayer. Why, who are we that God should think of us so tenderly, giving such fascinating and beautiful attention to the minutest details? True there have been the times when the pennies are measured out and all is done to make ends meet. But those tests have been, and still are times of rich blessing when pilgrims turn to the God who called them and whose responsibility they are. God's provisions have not yet failed, nor are they likely to in the future.

And what adventures could be told! A sense of humour saves the day – an absolutely essential part of a pilgrim's equipment. Take the time when after much prayer for funds one of the lady pilgrims was handed an envelope at the door by a handsome young man. 'Thank you', she said naïvely, 'thank you so much; we have been praying for this'. When she opened the envelope a little while later she found, not the expected pound notes, but a proposal of marriage! Or the time the four pilgrims were missioning and praying earnestly for those who attended the meetings. One man seemed particularly impressed and they concentrated prayer on him. Night after night he sat listening intently with his eyes glued to the girls as they sang and spoke. Then one day he appeared at the door of their lodgings and asked to speak to a particular pilgrim. She went down and the others dropped to their knees in earnest prayer that God would give wisdom in the conversation and save him. He confessed that he had a problem, a problem of the heart's affections, and the problem would be completely solved if the pilgrim would marry him. She escaped as best she could, darted up the stairs, and gasped, 'You can stop praying. It's not the Lord he wants, it's me!'

Pilgrims have to be quick-witted too. A pair of young lady pilgrims visited the country minister with a view to asking him if he would intimate the mission from his pulpit, and also to give him a kindly invitation to the meetings. 'Oh', said he, 'and are you going to conduct a mission, and preach? How old are you?' She promptly answered: 'Few and evil have the days of the years of my life been, and have not attained unto the days of the years of the life of my fathers in the days of their pilgrimage'.

'Lord', was a pilgrim's closing prayer, 'if there are any in the meeting tonight who still do not know Thee, bless them with a sleepless night'. The meetings continued and several came to the Saviour. Six months later he received a letter from a lady in that town. 'You may not remember praying that prayer', she said as she reminded him of the benediction, 'but it happened to me. My sins rose like a mountain and I could not sleep a wink. I was unable to attend the meeting the next night, but the following night I came, and the Lord Jesus Christ saved my soul. You may remember pointing me to the Saviour. I went home and had another sleepless night for very joy of what had happened!'

It's worth it all! The joys and the sorrows, the blessings and the buffetings, the happiness and the hardships mingle together as the pilgrims 'praise, pray and peg-away'.

Here is a farmer called to be a pilgrim. He is out in the wind and the rain seeking the lost for Jesus. Here is a young lady who has seen ten years in the Master's service. Her father owns five farms but she has one burning passion ruling her life – people must come to Christ.

Here is a sculptor with high recommendations from his professors, but now he is involved in moulding the lives of men and women for God. Here is a businessman, a teacher, a nursing sister – professional people; here is an artisan, a joiner, a welder, a chef. Why did they leave their lucrative pursuits and enter such an active sphere of service? Why? The love of Christ constrains them. They cannot keep silent nor remain inactive when the lost are all around them. They must tell them, and as they see things from the viewpoint of eternity, their values change and they are thrust out into the service of God.

Jesus, said, 'I *must* be about my Father's business', 'I *must* work the works of Him that sent Me', 'other sheep I have . . . them also I *must* bring', 'I *must* preach in other cities also for thereto am I sent'. There was a *must* in the life of Jesus, a big compelling spirit, a divine constraint which urged Him on to accomplish man's salvation on the Cross. He died that men might live. The more we are controlled by this sacrificial spirit of Christ, so much the more will we be prepared to die to our ideals and plans, to our very dearest aspirations and heart-felt desires, that men might be saved.

It is this spirit which caused that missionary statesman Oswald J. Smith to say, when he was but a young man, 'I will give my life for service in any part of the world, and in any capacity that God wills that I should labour'. It is this spirit which separates young people from self-indulgent materialism and lukewarm worldliness to lay their lives at the Master's feet to do whatever He desires and to go wherever He directs. It is this spirit which sends them into the often hard and unresponsive villages of the land bearing the Word of life. It is the sight of the suffering Saviour that makes all the difference. The tremendous story of the Cross grips men's hearts and stirs them to action. Then it is no longer sacrifice, but a privilege, a delight, an ecstasy of giving the best we have to the One we love the most. Then it is no longer a question of 'Must I go', but one of 'May I go?' Then we can say with Isaiah, 'Here am I, send me!' May God save us from getting used to the tramp, tramp, tramp of men and women going to hell, and send us out with burdened, broken, burning hearts to tell of His great salvation. 'Woe is me' said Paul, 'if I preach not the Gospel'.

After many years of service the Mission has proved itself to be an organization on which God has set His seal, and which He has greatly used to the salvation of thousands of souls. The results have had to be acknowledged for they speak for themselves.

The messages of the pilgrims were direct, warning, simple, encouraging. They used homely illustrations; they moved among the people; they talked their language and understood their problems. People more easily unburdened their hearts to those who got alongside them, and who on many occasions actually helped them physically with their work, either on the farm or in the home. 'I was changing nappies at one o'clock in the morning', says one. 'I watched all night at the bedside of the old man who was sick, and the family was able to get some sleep', says another. 'I helped them load the truck', says another. These things were done in the course of duty as an expression of Christian love. The people recognized the love and responded to it. But more than anything else, God was with the pilgrims.

There was an unction, a power from heaven, that indescribable 'something' which rests on a preacher who has waited in the presence of God. The pilgrims prayed, and prayed, and prayed. It was there that they were equipped with holy unction. It was there that they gathered their munitions. It was there that their hearts were set alight with holy fire. Prayer was the driving force, the strength, the power, the glory of the whole work. They knew the Scripture which says, 'He that goeth forth and weepeth bearing precious seed, shall doubtless come again with rejoicing, bringing his sheaves with him' (Ps 126:6).

Abraham prayed for Lot in Sodom and prevailed, Jacob wrestled all night with the angel and prevailed, Moses stood in the gap for Israel and prevailed. Elijah prayed on Mount Carmel and won a mighty victory. What power there is in persevering, believing prayer!

John Wesley declared, 'God does nothing but by prayer, and everything with it!' Jonathan Edwards said, 'There is no way that Christians, in a private capacity, can do so much to promote the work of God and advance the Kingdom of Christ as by prayer'. The pilgrims prayed. In the Name of their mighty Sovereign Lord they challenged the citadels of Satan, and in so many cases, saw them fall.

> 'High are the cities that dare our assault;
> Strong are the barriers that call us to halt;
> March we on fearless and down they must fall,
> Vanquished by faith in Him, far above all.'

This was the fighting spirit and language of their hearts. From the presence of God they came, and because of this, their meetings were fresh and vital, their words had a cutting edge, their messages had barbed arrows. God spoke through these young people in the power of the Holy Spirit.

It was the dying John Wesley who said, 'the best of all is, God is with us'. That too might be said of many a conference, of many a convention or campaign. If the presence of God were to be withdrawn, the Faith Mission would cease to exist, for there is no great organization behind it. The Faith Mission lives in God, and if God were not known and sensed in its activities, it would simply fold up. How important for the pilgrims to live in the presence of God; to live holy, blameless, undefiled lives. How vital for the workers to walk in the Spirit, to keep their lives transparent, to maintain an intimate relationship and deep communion with God. Here lies the Mission's power and its very life.

It is in God's holy fellowship that purity is maintained and it is His holy presence operating through the worker which accomplishes His purposes. Without it no spiritual work will prosper, 'for it is God which worketh in you both to will and to do of His good pleasure' (Phil 2:13). God's holiness maintains a work in its vitality and power. When the channels are clear, He works, establishing a holy Church, a useful Body and a spotless Bride. We cannot afford not to be holy!

CHAPTER 14

Sustained, Inspired, Sent!

Meanwhile the work continued and the years rolled on. For the second time this century the country was to be plunged into the horrors of war. The sad and terrible days of the last great European War with its hideous tale of suffering and death were about to be repeated. The war overshadowed everything and disrupted life in all its facets and activities both secular and religious.

'Young men engaged in our work', wrote the editor of *Bright Words*, 'have been acknowledged to be doing a work of national importance, and have not been called up'. But inevitably the war had its harrowing effects upon pilgrim life. The number of pilgrims decreased. In 1938 there were ninety-nine pilgrims in the work and at the end of 1945 there were seventy-five. Difficulties were encountered in many ways and in many areas of life.

Food and clothing were rationed; restrictions were placed on travel; some areas were closed to any but the residents, and workers were not permitted to enter. In some districts, such as East Anglia, it was almost impossible at times to hold meetings. The general dislocation of life and work and the movement of evacuees hindered evangelism. People did not attend meetings beause of the strange circumstances and a general feeling of apprehension and uncertainty. All this was intensified by the black-outs, the dark roads, the lack of petrol.

Public facilities for travel were reduced and awkward, and conventions of long standing had to be cancelled. Permits had to be obtained for lengthy journeys and there was a ban on unrestricted travel between Britain and Ireland. Even when this ban was lifted at the close of the war, it took some time for smooth sailing programmes to be established.

These were days of tension and trial, and in the midst of it all came the King's call to prayer. In 1944 he said, 'I desire solemnly to call my people to prayer and dedication. We are not unmindful of our own shortcomings, past and present. We shall not ask that God may do our will, but that we may be enabled to do the will of God. Not one of us is too busy, too young, or too old to play their part in a nation-wide – perhaps a world-wide – vigil of prayer.'

Would that in the spiritually dark days of 1986 we would hear again from high places, either political or ecclesiastical, such a stirring national call to turn to God! Would that our leaders had spiritual vision to see the calamitous slide of the nation. Materialism is on the march, Communism is on the march, Islam is on the march, and while the nation sleeps, they rob us of our great Christian heritage. Oh, for a voice to ring out and turn men and women back to God.

In the midst of the turmoil and tragedy of the war, the work of the Mission was amazingly sustained. Missions were held, many under difficult circumstances, and God was pleased to bless in a remarkable way. Throughout the period the words, 'God has supplied our needs,' 'our needs have been fully met', and similar expressions are constantly repeated. Had they received more, they would of course have used it to forward the work even further, yet they lived within the income provided and saw a great work done.

The Mission itself had suffered through the war years. Lack of adequate travel meant lack of communication, and the Mission was in danger of losing its cohesion and unity. The Irish work could grow away from the Scottish and English work, and a new inspiration to united service was necessary. The war had ruptured normal communications, and for five years the Perth Convention, where the Scottish and English workers had gathered annually, had not been held. Larne Convention too was discontinued for five years.

The Bangor Convention however, surged ahead despite the war years with 3,000 gathering on the Easter Monday of 1943. The Mission needed to be united in a new way and sense again, as a whole work, the aims and principles which brought it into being. So, the Glenada Conference was born.

The whole mission gathered before Easter in 1946, at the YWCA home 'Glenada', Newcastle, Co Down, Northern Ireland. Not since 1919 had the whole mission gathered like this for a time of unhurried waiting upon God. 'Over all these gatherings brooded the tenderness of God. The messages unfolded leading us first to the conscious comfort of His presence and then to a place of heart-searching and abasement. From there we were led to the Cross, and to many came a fresh relevation of the power of that precious blood. More than once there came a crisis in the times of prayer when we were able to receive the Holy Spirit afresh for all the will of God to be wrought out in our lives. None of us will ever forget those hallowed days of revelation. The Mission, individually and collectively, needed such a transfiguration experience, and the Lord came to us at Glenada in a way beyond our expectation or deserving. We give Him praise for the new touch of fire, the renewal of our commission, and the remarkable unity of spirit and purpose of which we were very conscious'.

The *Pilgrim News*, a letter circulated each week among the workers giving up-to-date reports of the work, shows a constant stream of blessing in a number of areas particularly in some parts of Ireland.

John Farquhar, who worked with several different pilgrims during a period of two years from September 1946 to September 1948 saw God blessing in a remarkable way. Missions conducted in Co Antrim were very well attended with a great sense of God in the meetings bringing many under conviction of sin and to salvation in Christ. Many Christians were revived and transformed in this gracious move of the Spirit. At one place they counselled and prayed with sixteen members of one family connection who trusted God for salvation or for other spiritual needs.

In two tent missions he and his fellow-pilgrims saw 137 people turn to God, mainly for salvation. These missions were greatly used by God and released new life into the whole area. Mission followed mission and people just kept coming to Christ. In the midst of it all he was sent to Co Cork, Eire, where another twenty-five trusted the Lord. In all, in this fruitful period, they pointed over 550 people to Christ, the majority of whom trusted the Lord Jesus as Saviour. From these missions fourteen young people entered the Faith Mission Bible College, eleven of whom were in training at the same time in the 1948/49 session.

Recording bare facts like these brings a sense of amazement, wonder and longing, but can never impart that sense of the divine which characterizes the meeting in which God comes and takes the field. How dreadful is His presence. What awe and stillness fill the place. The unsaved in the community are often gripped by fear. Men and women see the majesty and glory of God and can only bow at His feet in brokenness, wonder, love and praise. The mind is convinced of His saving power, the emotions are stirred, the will is submitted, the life is surrendered – God has conquered. They come in repentance, and receive, instead of judgement, free grace and eternal life. Gratitude fills their hearts and becomes the irrepressible fountain of consecration and service. Men and women are born again in the atmosphere of eternity and are spoiled for everything else.

The suggestion of a Former Pilgrims' Fellowship came from Helen Gibb who had pioneered the work in Canada, and who was at that time in charge of the YWCA at Southport. In 1947 the Fellowship, managed entirely by former pilgrims, was formed, and, linked together by an occasional long newsletter made up of contributions from former pilgrims everywhere, it has been a source of comfort, interest and inspiration. 'How very interesting to hear that

Jean, with whom I worked in the North, is now a mother of three children'; 'how thrilling to hear of Jack's good work in Africa'; 'John is now in South America'; so the comments run, and the fellowship is kept alive.

In 1960 it had 257 members, some in lands far away, yet all were united in the spirit and purpose of those former pilgrim days. 'It was the first time I met her', said one, 'but when she said that she had been a pilgrim, we felt an enormous sense of belonging to each other in the service of God. We had both known what it meant to bear the burden of a campaign, and had both led souls to Jesus. We were one'. And what conferences they held. 'Better even than our old pilgrim meetings', said another.

Yet numbers have declined. Some of the old warriors have been promoted to glory, and the increasing cost of travel has prevented many from attending their annual conferences. The FPF however forms a very useful link with the Mission encouraging fellowship and stimulating prayer. It continues today under the presidency of the Rev A. Fraser of Birmingham.

CHAPTER 15

Prayer Unions and Conventions

The following words are printed on the Faith Mission Prayer Union membership card:

> 'The Prayer Union, started in 1887, aims to unite in fellowship and love the converts of the Mission and others in sympathy, who desire to be wholly the Lord's, and to seek first the Kingdom. Members are expected to pray for each other, for the work of the Mission, and for an outpouring of the Holy Spirit on the whole Church of Christ.'

The Prayer Unions had grown from those early days in Fife and from that mighty march through Dunfermline in 1888 which celebrated the first anniversary of the formation of Prayer Unions, to a large body of people which stood with the pilgrims in their battles. Like a wise master builder John George Govan had realized that the fruit of evangelism had to be conserved, and that prayer was the one great factor which would do it. This led to the formation of the Faith Mission Prayer Union. At the outset of his great work, John Wesley had stood before the same problem and the Methodist Class meeting, where groups gather for prayer and mutual encouragement, was the result. The Faith Mission issued a membership card which entailed at that time, a small charge, and every year there is the happy event of the Annual Rejoining. It was made very clear that the Prayer Union, like the Mission itself, was not a sect, and was to be maintained strictly on interdenominational lines. Undoubtedly the Prayer Unions have been the backbone of the work. The members have prayed and stood with the pilgrims down the years. They have been glad partners in evangelism for they have fostered fellowship, and encouraged converts. Many a Christian has fearfully uttered his first words of public prayer in these meetings, and many an 'Amen' of hearty encouragement has been given by those strong in the faith. Christians have gained experience at these meetings as they have helped converts with their teething problems, and others have had to delve more deeply into the Word as they prepared to lead Bible studies or speak at meetings. Some developed skills in leading meetings or in singing solos or duets. It was a training ground, a place of development and joy, a place of fellowship and strength, and where necessary and possible the pilgrims formed Prayer Unions.

'Some Prayer Unions have gone on very well', said the Chief, 'and others are not satisfactory'.

From country districts there is apt to be a continuous emigration, and this of course affects the meeting. Some folk would become involved in other aspects of God's work and would therefore not be able to attend the Prayer Union. Yet the pilgrims, knowing the value of prayer backing everywhere, encouraged the formation of prayer groups. During times of blessing these would be strong and the numbers of prayer groups would increase. During 1960, there were 456, and in 1964 there were 511 Prayer Unions.

Today many Prayer Unions are carried on by the faithful few who stand with the pilgrims in their conflicts and conquests, but there are also many Prayer Unions which are numerically strong. They have seen young people go from their fellowships to the Bible College and to the ends of the earth. Thank God for those who pray! There are over 400 of these invaluable groups all over the British Isles today. The power and effect of their prayers can never be estimated. The battle to win men and women to Christ is fierce, and more than ever before, these praying groups are needed.

It is not an easy thing to pray. There is a price to be paid, a price of curbed freedom, of resolute concentration, of agonizing supplication. To stay in the presence of God baring your soul to His searching gaze costs everything! It is easy to slip away and to stay away from the prayer meeting. It costs too much. The one who prays however, cannot but be transformed, for prayer is a purifying medium. When we take time with God prayer becomes a transforming exercise. Here is the secret of the burning heart and the shining face. Here is the open secret of spiritual growth. Prayer is a rewarding ministry. Not only are its results felt at the point at which prayer is focussed, but the one who prays is enormously enriched. By spending time in prayer we do not decrease our activity but we increase our productivity and accomplish vastly more. Let us use this great weapon of prayer which God has given us. Pray on! Pray on!

No one knows the value of the Prayer Unions more than the District Superintendent whose responsibility it is to visit them regularly. How eagerly his visit is anticipated by little groups of people in isolated places, who otherwise have little in the way of spiritual help. To him too falls the responsibility of arranging and planning for the pilgrims allocated to his particular district, keeping in touch with them during the course of their missions, giving advice, counsel and encouragement. To him comes the task of maintaining contact with Christians and converts after the mission is over. He arranges conferences and conventions and keeps the whole work going on to fulfil its God-given responsibility, to reach the lost with the gospel in the power of the Spirit.

Wherever there has been blessing the converts need care, and as a result conferences sprang up all over. People gathered for a day, with two or three meetings at some places, or for an afternoon at others. Sometimes tea would be served between the afternoon and evening sessions, or perhaps just an evening session would be held. These conferences have been greatly blessed all over the country and many people carry fragrant memories of the times when the Word was spoken with power and when they were so encouraged by the warm and happy fellowship. Today over 250 of these conferences are held by the Mission each year. Some are annual, some are monthly, and some quarterly. Circular letters from the District Headquarters tell of the progress of the work and announce the conference dates and times.

There are conventions as well – longer periods of ministry where people often come and stay in various house-parties and attend the meetings arranged. The Edinburgh Convention, held in September, and the Bangor Easter Convention are the main ones, but there are also other gatherings in the English Midlands, Fraserburgh and Londonderry, all held in May, Bandon (Co Cork) held in June, the Irish Midlands and Stornoway held in August, Stranraer and Larne in September, and Ballymena in October. Thrilling stories could be told of each convention as Christians gather together. How God blessed the early efforts of the pilgrims in those most southerly and westerly parts of Ireland!

The Perth Convention as the main Scottish Convention continued to exercise a strong influence. It was moved to Edinburgh in 1957 and it is to this convention that the Scottish and English pilgrims come after the summer work. Pilgrim meetings are held for a few days before the public convention begins. These meetings have been the lifeblood of the Mission down the years. Here the pilgrims have an opportunity to wait on the Lord, to hear His voice speaking to them as servants of God, to take stock and to humble themselves before God. Messages are given and prolonged periods of prayer are held. Sometimes meals are set aside as workers continue in prayer when it has pleased God to come on occasions with melting power. Sometimes He comes with dynamic authority and at others He just steals into a meeting. But when He comes, what brokenness, what healing, what inspiration, what joy He brings. Pilgrims need challenge and encouragement, tenderness and grace, and He is there to meet all their needs. Refreshed by His presence, gladdened by His ministry, recommissioned by His Word, they are ready for full involvement in the convention that follows.

How these conventions have rung with the praises of heaven down the years. What singing! How often the meeting is lifted from the natural to the supernatural by the glad bursts of acclamation from the children of God. What a great contribution the testimonies have made over the years as deeply spiritual men and women have told of God's grace and power. And what of the solos, duets and singing groups! 'She sang the presence of God into the meetings', commented someone at a convention. But they have been saying that for a century, and still the Holy Spirit endorses the consecrated singing of His dedicated servants. The secret of the conventions is the presence of God, and the glory of his presence must ever fill and thrill God's waiting people.

What of the Bangor Convention? It has been and still is the major convention of the Faith Mission. Look at the coaches, numbers of them standing at the bus station on Easter Monday with people from all over Ireland stepping out and walking to the open churches. Look at the people pouring out of the station. They are coming to the Faith Mission Bangor Convention. In the fifties and sixties five large churches were engaged for the fifteen meetings held on Easter Monday. Speakers' names and the churches in which they are preaching are on several boards in the town and people attend the churches of their choice. Five thousand convention-going people thronged Bangor in those days. The sad troubles of Northern Ireland together with the development of other church conventions have lessened the numbers somewhat, but thousands still stream in on this great day of the feast. Godly men from a great variety of places and from different denominations have ministered the word of God over the years. How rich the biblical ministry has been! At the special 'pilgrim meetings' on Monday afternoons, pilgrims give stirring reports and relate moving incidents from the year's work. These 'report-back' meetings are always highlights and the pilgrims' passion and sacrificial spirit so often grips the congregation, preparing the way for the message which is to follow. Young people come in large numbers. In 1985 more than 200 young folk were accommodated in church halls and were cared for throughout the convention. The thrill of seeing the people come, of meeting old friends and of renewing aquaintances, the joy of marching on the Sunday morning at sunrise from the church down to the seafront, led by the Salvation Army Band, singing resurrection songs and choruses, all make the convention a memorable one. And let us not forget the great missionary meeting on Tuesday afternoon. Six or seven missionaries tell of their work and are followed by a stirring challenge from the Word. Some will never forget those meetings, for it was there that God called them into His service. The people leave Bangor so often having met with God, and are ready with new inspiration to meet the demands of the days ahead.

One of the very lovely things about the Faith Mission is its openness to the mission fields of the world. It has always encouraged those who wish to go and has constantly pointed young people to God's service wherever that may be. The first two to leave the first Irish Prayer Union at Glenvar, Blackrock, did not go into the ranks of the Mission, but one went to China, and the other to D. L. Moody's work in America. From the very outset the Training Home was said to train workers for home and abroad. Down the years young people have worked for a few years in the Mission and then have gone to the ends of the earth with numerous missionary societies. While their loss to the Mission is sometimes keenly felt, the leaders rejoice that a wider field is being served. Others far beyond the borders of this country are benefiting from the College training. Principles of holy living and spiritual harvesting learned in active involvement in Faith Mission work are being transmitted to many others today.

From the fifth year the Mission has had a Foreign Fund, and its Holiness or Deeper Life Conventions have always had a missionary emphasis as well. In 1911 money from the missionary meetings at conventions and any money ear-marked for missions was sent to over twenty approved missionary societies. John George Govan wrote: 'Interest in the foreign field has increased among us throughout the year. We are glad of this, both for the sake of the heathen world lying in darkness, and for the enlargement of hearts and sympathies which it brings, as distinguished from the selfish and sectarian spirit which is interested only in "my little corner". We "seek first" not sect, denomination, or even Mission, but "the kingdom", and that kingdom is world extensive'. In 1927 nine left the Mission for the foreign field and five others for the home field in different areas of service. In 1938 we read, 'in a large measure the Faith Mission is a training ground for those going abroad. Many missionaries in all parts of the world gladly bear witnesss to what their pilgrim days meant to them'. There have been at least 300 pilgrims who became foreign missionaries, to say nothing of the many who were saved through the Mission and who went abroad without training at the F.M. Bible College. Over 100 former pilgrims went into the ministry in the British Isles, but many others who came to Christ through the Mission became ministers in their own denominations, again without Faith Mission training.

In 1938 the Mission, with a total income of £4,129.00, passed on no less than £400 to the mission field. At nearly every convention there is a special offering for missions and this is gladly given, despite the fact that the Mission has often to budget very carefully to ensure that the convention covers itself financially. The Bangor Convention alone in 1985 gave almost £4,000 to missions. Perhaps this unselfish attitude, this generous spirit, and the fact that the Mission recognizes and acknowledges the value of servants of God world-wide and lends a helping hand to them in their task, is one of the reasons why God is still pleased to bless it in its own gatherings in the homeland.

CHAPTER 16

Tenacity, Expectancy, Victory!

Between the years 1949 and 1953 the Spirit of God was poured out in a most remarkable way on the Isle-of-Lewis in the Western Isles of Scotland. The instrument whom God used in this movement was Rev Duncan Campbell who was at the time a member of the Faith Mission and was later appointed Principal of the Bible College. This revival is known in many parts of the world as 'The Lewis Awakening', and its news has been the means of stirring Christians everywhere to pray that God would again visit His people in great power and blessing. At the time, Mr Campbell wrote a small booklet outlining some of the features of the movement, and this has been included as an addendum to this centenary volume.

This revival was undoubtedly the most significant event in the Faith Mission work at that time. However, while revival fires burned in Lewis, the Mission work was continuing with much blessing throughout the country.

Through the years missions have been held in a great variety of meeting-places, churches, schools, public halls, Orange halls (in Ireland), barns, lofts, farm-kitchens, tents (in summer), and many other places. When, for some reason or other, meeting places were difficult to obtain, the answer seemed to lie in 'portable halls'. These are sectional halls, capable of being erected and dismantled without undue difficulty, giving access to places where no meeting place is available, and where missions could not otherwise be held. Used from the turn of the century they were always useful, but particularly so in the fifties and sixties when they met a real need. In fact, in 1962, there were twenty-two of these halls in use.

In summer, tents served a useful purpose, and in the earlier days, there were five tents in constant use in the summer months in Ireland. These, although used for many years were not really suited to the changeable climatic conditions. Wind, rain, cold weather and tents are not happy partners, and while there were some great and blessed missions under canvas, the tent missions had their problems and never constituted a major part of Faith Mission evangelism.

Another problem was that of obtaining suitable lodgings for the pilgrims in many of the places to which they went. This was solved to some extent by the use of caravans. The caravans used at the Mission's beginnings were primitive and cumbersome in comparison to the luxurious 'homes on wheels' of the present day. In the early sixties there were twenty-five caravans in use at the one time. Some were purchased by small donations coming in gradually, and some were gifts by individual donors. Caravans have certainly met a real need as pilgrims have moved from place to place ministering the Word.

Those who were not fortunate enough to have accommodation in the form of caravans had some interesting adventures. At times the pilgrims lived in beautiful homes with their every need supplied – God sometimes gives lovely surprises along the pilgrim pathway – but at others they had to 'rough it'. Sometimes they had to scrub the place out before it was fit for human habitation. 'You keep the diseases away from us Lord, and we'll scrub for all we're worth,' said one as she cleaned a dirty disused cottage. There has been many a laugh at the variety of meals produced by the men pilgrims living in caravans and cooking for themselves – but they have survived!

'Isn't it blessed', the Chief had once said, 'when you go into a village to be able to say to yourself, "I am here for one thing, and one thing alone, and that is to see souls saved"'! In one area we read that the visiting was such a blessing to the people, and 'the reading of the Scriptures in the homes was greatly appreciated'. 'I didn't know what you meant when you spoke about the visiting being a drain on you!' said one who happened to accompany a pilgrim one day, 'but now I know! Why this *is* the work'. How often in the homes where the issue cannot be side-stepped, people are brought face to face with their spiritual need, and yield to the Saviour. For the pilgrims it is ministry all the time, in the hall, or in the home. They don't waste too much time on the weather or on world events. They are only there for a short period, and time is precious. They must confront people as tactfully yet as clearly as possible with the fact of their eternal destiny.

A middle-aged man had lived a respectable, upright but self-righteous life. He attended church and read the Scriptures regularly, yet these things meant little to him. Early in the mission his two daughters were saved, causing him amazement, and then deep concern in his quest for what he called 'the real thing'. At last the light dawned and he trusted Christ. As the pilgrims left his home, he said, 'I have got the real thing at last'. The visit was fruitful. 'Do you mean to tell me', said an indignant gentleman, 'that all my church-going, all my religion, all my good living does not count before God? If anyone's a Christian in this valley, I am'. Patiently they reasoned with him as he sat gazing out of the window at his beautiful farm. It meant more than one visit, but at last he was convinced of his lost condition before God, and they all rejoiced together as he yielded his life to the Saviour. 'Come and see me at home', have been the words many have whispered on the way out of a meeting – and the worker has rejoiced. That visit will be, oh, so significant.

Two old people had been led to the Lord in their home by a pilgrim on his earlier visit to the village. Now he and his fellow-worker were passing by and they stopped outside the humble little home. There was not much time but the old people would surely appreciate a visit. Instruction was simple, earnest, loving and respectful. How God stole into that little room! The pilgrims left with red eyes and grateful hearts, for God's presence was so precious.

Visiting 'is the work'. It is not visiting for pleasure, but it is visiting with purpose. They did not come into the area just to make friends, but to win people to Jesus. This is the uppermost thought and the driving passion, and this takes them from one home to another telling the glad story of redemption.

In 1955, 26,000 hours were spent visiting the people in their homes. Today visiting is still a major part of the pilgrim's life and ministry. Mornings are spent in prayer, study, and preparation for their evenings' messages, and afternoons are nearly always given to meeting the people in their own homes.

On they go, these pilgrims, cheerfully enduring the constant strain of attacking the enemy's kingdom, and with much soul travail seeing men and women delivered from his power. 'At one place on *Skye*,' we read in 1951, 'we saw a real stirring of the Spirit. In another we had good meetings but not with the same outward response although some did find peace in believing'. In *Co Wicklow*, Ireland, comes the news that year of 'the outpouring of His Spirit in our midst. Numbers saved and backsliders restored'. In *West Calder*, Scotland, too, the same year, we hear that 'God seemed to make His presence known right from the start of the mission. We were conscious that He was working in a marked way. A number of young people and adults trusted Christ for salvation.'

At *Tullygarley* in Ireland zeal and earnestness had subsided considerably before the pilgrims came and after a hard four weeks some advised them to close the mission, but it continued and God began to bless. A wonderful sense of God's presence prevailed and the mission went on for eight weeks. Many were saved and Christians mightily blessed. It was a great campaign.

'God has saved me,' said a young convert. 'The members of my family are all unbelievers, and when I started speaking about Christ, they really thought that I was mentally ill and sent me to a psychiatrist. I hope that I convinced him that I did not need a doctor, but that perhaps he needed a spiritual one!' 'I've known for years what I should do', said a lady, 'but it is so hard to let worldly things go, and I feel they must go if I am to be converted'. The surrender was made and another found peace. 'I thought I couldn't live without them,' said a lassie whose life was given to the dance-hall and every kind of amusement, 'but I have found Christ, and now I find that I don't want these things. I have something far better!' 'Oh yes, I have often thought that I needed to get saved, but have never taken the step', the old lady said. 'You have been thinking about it for eighty-three years; don't you think it's time you did something about it?' the pilgrim replied. And there in her home as they talked, the Lord drew so near. She came to Him just as she was and trusted Him as her Saviour.

'Don't go and visit that man,' the people warned. 'He'll curse you till you're out of his sight'. But they went, and he was as meek as a lamb. 'Well, I might come to the meetings, I'll see', he said. Two nights later he came with his wife and two teenage children. They sat in a row near the back, his chin thrust out at a defiant angle. The next night they were all back again, and disappeared before the benediction had been pronounced. The third night they were back once more. What a night! God came into the midst. 'Are you born again? Do you have assurance of salvation? When did you come to Christ? Oh, come to Him now!' The pilgrim's stirring appeal rang out clearly, but so tenderly. They came to Jesus that night; all four of them! The pilgrim wept as he prayed with the repentant and later rejoicing foursome. Six months later he received a letter from the mother. 'Our home is so changed', she said, 'my husband has family prayers every evening with us all now – and he prays so beautifully.'

Tenacity and purpose are so necessary in pilgrim life, and how two of the men needed just those qualities: 'It was the middle of winter and wintry conditions prevailed with ice and snow as we commenced our mission', they reported. 'Some of the people were opposed to our coming, others were indifferent and a few seemed interested. We lodged in a little unoccupied house which became known as the "Bachelors' Manse". The Public Hall was rented for the meetings, but for the first fortnight few locals attended, and it seemed as though we would have to close. One morning, however, when we were unable to have the use of the hall, we walked through the snow to a small cluster of houses some miles away for a cottage meeting. While visiting these we made contact with a man who was popular socially, but had no time for God. His wife was prepared to attend, but the arrival of unexpected visitors prevented her. Having heard about the difficult times we were having, and knowing that on a night such as this there would, in all probability, not be many at the meeting, he decided to come in order to encourage us. That night God dealt with him, and some nights later we had the joy of leading both him and his wife to the Lord. From that night onwards interest seemed to increase daily and others found the Saviour too. On the closing night of the mission there were between 200 and 300 present and there was only standing room. One man commented that it was the largest gospel meeting in that area in his memory. We give God all the glory. Initial apparent defeat was transformed into glorious victory.'

'Soulwinning is the primary work of the Faith Mission,' the Chief had said long ago, 'and unless it continues to be a soul-saving agency, it does not deserve to exist'. The pilgrims were fulfilling their calling. Story after wonderful story can be told as the drama of pilgrim life continues to unfold.

How the people appreciate the pilgrims' whole-hearted devotion. This tribute comes from Scotland in 1957: 'The indisputable evidence of changed lives testifies to the fruitfulness of the work. The pilgrims have worked with selfless devotion. They have a firmly crystallized purpose. With a single eye to God's glory, they labour faithfully, caring nothing for the applause of the world but much for the advancement of the cause of Christ. Fearlessly, armed with the power of the Holy Spirit, they brave the attacks of the enemy of souls, attacks which are sometimes indicated by open eruptions of hostility, at other times creeping along in veiled insidious guise. We have no doubt that to such consecrated servants of the Master, acceptance as humble instruments in His hand, seems more to be desired than the heritage of earth's greatest king.' Paul says, 'they glorified God in me'. It is the life that counts more than the words that are spoken, and this draws men and women to God.

There was always, and is always the longing for an outpouring of the Spirit. At the close of 1950 the Irish Director wrote, 'There have been showers, and a moving, a preparation, and there is a spirit of expectancy abroad. Surely another year cannot pass without the visitation of God in mighty power.' Throughout the Mission the pilgrims continued to work hard and to wait long upon God for a revelation of His power, and here and there the Lord gave gracious indications of His blessing.

In 1955 two lady pilgrims, Misses Wilson and Morrison, were sent to the Isle-of-Tiree a place where the pilgrims had reaped abundant harvests in times past. They worked for seven discouraging weeks with very little interest in the work. But they prayed! One morning as they were on their knees together, they prayed right through to victory. 'The devil's on the run', said one, 'the devil's on the run!' They were so filled with glory that they laughed in the presence of God. It was the laugh of faith and victory. They had touched the throne. From that night on God worked! There was the sound of an abundance of rain. From one place to another on that island, but twelve miles long and six miles wide, they went. The missions were 'great' and the pilgrims endeared themselves to the people as they missioned. Even the ungodly said, 'This must be the hand of God'.

When the District Superintendent visited the island he commented, 'There is no doubt that the Lord has been working on Tiree. The atmosphere of the place, which was thronging with the converts of recent missions, was wonderful'.

The pilgrims went on to Lochmaddy on the island of N. Uist together with two others. They were the first pilgrims for a very long time to visit the island and at first folk were suspicious of them. They used the village hall, and night after night they preached. The spiritual atmosphere deepened and after several weeks, the break came. Suddenly they began to come to Christ. The local barman was saved. Instead of the bar being crowded and packed to capacity on Saturday nights, few entered its doors. On one Saturday evening only seven men were at the bar and the hotel manager was concerned that his whisky was still on the shelves! The Spirit of God was being outpoured on the community. What wonderful times of blessing!

On to Sollas, they went. Acquiring the school they were arranging the benches in a way to accommodate as many people as possible when the headmaster came in. 'There's no need for that', he said, 'not many will come to the meetings'. But as he spoke, a word came to one of the pilgrims like a bolt from the blue, 'I will work, and who shall let it?' (Is 43:13). In the end, the side room had to be opened and the little ones sat on the floor in the front. A bus brought folk from other places to the meetings, and God blessed in a remarkable way. One night the bus was so full that its springs broke!

On they went to the next place where five men had arranged to meet and discuss how best they could upset the meetings. As one of them walked to his 'council of war' he saw another two carrying planks to the school hall. 'What are you doing?' he asked. 'Don't ask questions, just lend a hand', was the gruff reply.

At the school they quickly made the seats and arranged them in the hall – for the meetings that they wanted to prevent! 'We couldn't let the girls do it alone', they explained, chafing under the indignity of having been on hand at just the wrong time. 'These men, Lord,' prayed the girls, 'are the leaders in all the worldly activities here. Please save these five fine young men'. And all five were saved, in fact they were among the first to be saved in this yet another move of God's Spirit. 'Not even at worldly functions have I seen so many cars and buses,' was the comment at this mission. The newspapers seized the story and it was soon in bold type, much to the displeasure of the pilgrims. The Spirit of God went before them from place to place. There were seasons of refreshing from the presence of the Lord.

While the pilgrims were out in the fight, the Mission continued to be administered from Edinburgh. For forty years the General Headquarters had been at 262 Morrison Street, but eventually the Mission was given notice to vacate their premises. On 30th April 1952 it opened its new headquarters at 38 Coates Gardens, Edinburgh which it purchased. This proved a great blessing, for much more accommodation was now available than was afforded in the inadequate premises in Morrison Street. There was room for offices, the bookroom, a meeting room capable of holding fifty people, and a flat at the top.

The mission's seventieth year, 1956, was encouraging with 121 workers on the staff, although nine retired during the year. Their places were filled from the College and the numbers were sustained. In 1952 there were thirty-eight students in the College. Numbers were maintained, and in 1960 there were forty-four students in training.

Interest in conferences was high with 450 people attending the 749th Edinburgh Conference in 1957 held at Carrubber's Close Mission. Yet the Mission was now operating in a world which was increasingly secularized and more difficult to evangelize.

CHAPTER 17

The Changing Scene and a new Youth Emphasis

Times had changed. It was a new world. Pilgrim work in the sixties could not be compared with those early rugged days of physical hardship yet great spiritual blessing. Everybody knew then that the pilgrims were preaching the Word of God, and although some resisted violently, they were acknowledged and given a hearing. In the sixties and on to the present this resistance has given way to apathy and indifference. People are just not interested in the things of God. The god of this world has blinded the minds of those who do not believe.

Housing estates springing up all over are brick and concrete mission fields. Many have no evangelical witness and many have never been visited by Christian workers. Britain was changing, changing from a great Christian land which sent the gospel into earth's remotest corners to a land which today is itself in need of missionaries. Few people in these estates invited the workers into their homes, and they had to preach as they could on the doorsteps and trust that the tract pushed into an unwilling hand would speak to those who read it – 'please Lord, let them read it'. Some means had to be found to reach the people. Perhaps taking a census would help, so some workers ran off forms with various general questions leading on to those of a religious nature. This would at least keep the door open for a few minutes of conversation so that they could give something of the gospel. The villages, so picturesque and beautiful with their lovely patches of green lawn and flowers in such glorious profusion, were becoming hard and cold towards God. The people had no time for Him. Their lives were filled with the countless things that money can buy. They had never 'had it so good'. God was left out of their calculations. Both mother and father were working in so many homes and when they returned in the evenings they were in no mood to tolerate two religious 'cranks' at the door, nor were they inclined to go to any religious meeting. It would be much more comfortable to sit in an easy chair with the paper and mug of tea or beer and enjoy all that the TV had to offer. Numerous counter-attractions militated against the preaching of the gospel. Life was good, the church had faded out of their thinking and the children's religious education was totally neglected. This was certainly a change from the days when the children answered Moody's question on prayer with a recitation from the Shorter Catechism!

The authority of the Scriptures had been undermined by modernism, and there was not the recognition of God nor the reverence for divine things that there used to be. Formerly, the religious background had formed a foundation upon which to build, but how rare this is today. Coupled with a general lack of concern, there is also real ignorance of basic spiritual truths, so that often pilgrims come to those who are spiritually unprepared. The present day pilgrim in Scotland and England has to sow the seed – if he can get a hearing – before any harvest can be expected.

Once the village was a self-contained unit, and an evangelistic mission was quite an event which captured young and old. Now all this has changed with the modern means of communication and transport.

What of the lowering of moral and ethical standards? These have fallen dramatically and the Christian church has been so conditioned to foul language and the degradation of sex that the people hardly notice it nor raise their voices in protest. Evil is tolerated to a degree that would have horrified those of a former generation. Christians have been conditioned to a state of complacency. They shrug their shoulders and say, 'things are bad these days', and evil is allowed to increase and triumph.

The false cults, hardly known a hundred years ago, are not idle either, and into these housing estates they go. Sometimes the pilgrims arrive at a village or housing estate just after the Jehovah's Witnesses or the Mormons have been. People are thrown into confusion and it is very difficult to gain a hearing. And the cults win their converts too! Two pilgrims once knocked on a door. The woman opened it, listened for a moment, and then began to close the door in their faces, 'Wait,' said the one, 'We're not Jehovah's Witnesses'. 'Well I am', she replied as she slammed the door and left them standing on the doorstep!

A modern paraphrased version of the Bible gives a graphic description of these conditions: 'You may as well know this too Timothy, that in the last days it is going to be very difficult to be a Christian. For people will love only themselves and their money; they will be proud and boastful, sneering at God, disobedient to their parents, ungrateful to them, and thoroughly bad. They will be hardheaded and never give in to others; they will be constant liars and troublemakers and will think nothing of immorality. They will be rough and cruel, and sneer at those who try to be good. They will betray their friends; they will be hot-headed, puffed up with pride, and prefer good times to worshipping God'. (II Tim. 3:1–4).

In the sixties, Scotland still held on to some of the religion that had been instilled into the folk from their earliest days – but it was going. Ireland was still strongly active with meetings everywhere, and the spiritual temperature was maintained to a very large degree. *Bright Words* reported that 'not for a number of years has there been such widespread blessing in the Faith Mission field of service in Ireland as in the winter of 1959/60'. Yet the scene was changing, for in 1962 we read in connection with the work in all three countries, that there were 'fewer results than in many of the immediately preceding years'. England was losing its grip on spiritual things and was rapidly becoming a dreadfully needy mission field. In the midst of the continual decline pilgrims kept up their visiting and their meetings. In 1960 they prayed with 743 people who came to Christ for salvation. Those who professed conversion could no longer be reckoned in thousands, but in hundreds.

In January 1962 the President gave very interesting figures concerning the progress of the Mission over the seventy-five years of its existence, and in particular the last half of that period. In 1961, 583 people had professed conversion, which is one-fifth of the number recorded in 1924, when the Mission was half its age. There had been in those thirty-seven years a steady decline of visible results. This was serious and called for real heart-searching, yet while not wanting to make excuses for the decline in the number of those professing conversion through the years, it must be admitted that there were difficulties in 1961 which were unknown in earlier times.

It was to Yorkshire and the Midlands in the sixties that the Mission felt directed. There had been some previous work when an invitation to hold missions had come from a couple who had gone to live in Otley. She was a former pilgrim and they had already begun a Prayer-Union meeting in their home. A further invitation had come from a church in Birmingham.

The first mission was conducted by two ladies, Misses Dunlop and Totten, at Otley in November, 1947. Early in 1948 Miss Dunlop was joined by Miss Toft, and in later years these two were better known as Mrs E. Fox and Mrs D. Howden, wives of Faith Mission Superintendents. For the next few years missions were conducted by several workers, but during the fifties few workers could be spared for this field.

From 1959 onwards sister pilgrims again missioned in Yorkshire and the Midlands. The two who had been operating in the Highlands, Misses Wilson and Morrison, opened up the Midlands in particular. They persevered in unknown surroundings and numbers were converted. Prayer Unions were formed and conferences were arranged to which

Duncan Campell and other well-known preachers were invited. At one conference in Birmingham 450 people were thrilled to hear how God was working and responded warmly to the challenge of the Biblical preaching. Some said, 'these inspiring times remind us of the great days with Samuel Chadwick'. A number of young people entered the College from these missions at that time. 'God was in it all', said Albert Dale, 'and the move to Yorkshire and the Midlands was altogether in the will of God'.

Having done the groundwork, the Mission could move a man into the area as Superintendent, and in 1963 Mr and Mrs David Howden went to York to supervise the district from there. This was the second English district making a total of six districts in Scotland and England. The move to the Midlands was perhaps the most outstanding event of the sixties. The Mission had been greatly used in Scotland and Ireland, and been established in the revival times in East Anglia in the twenties, and now this was the first major thrust into central England.

Miss Morrison's services were in demand and in 1963 the Council released her for an itinerant ministry which took her throughout the British Isles and also to Canada and to Southern Africa. Her testimony concerning her involvement in revival was recorded in Canada at the Spring Conference of the Prairie Bible Institute and put to paper. This little book, formerly 'Hearken O Daughter', and later, 'I was saved in Revival', has enjoyed three editions.

The later part of the decade was a period of great change in the Mission leadership. The sudden death of Bill Black in Ireland and the retirement of Duncan Campbell both in 1967 necessitated changes. In 1968 John Eberstein retired and Albert Dale became Director and Treasurer of the whole work with John Farquhar from Ireland becoming Director for Scotland.

All this time the pilgrims were 'hard at it'. Chalmers, the great Scottish preacher, said of the early Methodists, 'they are all at it, and always at it!' This could well be said of the pilgrims. 'At it' they were from morning till night, giving themselves completely in the service of God. In 1945 the Archbishops' Commission on Evangelism produced a paper called 'Towards the Conversion of England' and at the beginning an excellent definition of evangelism is given: 'To evangelize is so to present Christ Jesus in the power of the Holy Spirit that men shall come to put their trust in God through Him, to accept Him as their Saviour, and to serve Him as their King in the fellowship of the church'. To evangelize is '*so* to present Christ Jesus', that they put their trust in Him. It is not just a listing of gospel facts or Scripture texts, but it is the skilful and purposeful transmission of truth in the Spirit's power, in order that it may be received and may transform the recipient. Oh for a greater grasp of Scriptural truth! Oh, for a clearer presentation! Oh, for the power of the Holy Spirit in the delivery of the message! The pilgrims were trusting God for all these things as they worked. In 1963 they held 236 missions and spent 30,100 hours visiting the people. The number of just over 100 pilgrims in the work was maintained throughout the decade and every now and again God was pleased to encourage the Mission with very good campaigns. In some meetings of the Stornoway Convention which developed after the 1949–53 revival, there was a very marked sense of God's presence.

While it was difficult to get the people to the meetings in Scotland and England, there were some very good missions in Ireland. At one, numbers rose to over 300 on the Sunday nights with over fifty coming to Christ for salvation. Pilgrims tried in every way to get to the people. They went to schools and in many cases were allowed to address the assembly or to take a number of the Scripture classes. They worked through the churches, and through any organization that could gain them an entry. The message had to be proclaimed, but more than that, the message had to reach the people.

The people thronged the holiday centres, and some of

these places were fruitful fields of labour. Thousands streamed to Newcastle, Co Down, N. Ireland and pilgrims preached to hundreds on the promenade. *Life Indeed* magazine with its gospel emphasis in the summer months, was sold by the thousands to the milling crowds. It was estimated that at the Newcastle Open Air Campaign in 1968, 25,000 people heard the gospel. It was a very exhausting eight weeks for the pilgrims who were really 'whacked' at the end of it. Tired but triumphing they emerged to fight other battles and to see other victories won.

What a joy it is when in the battle, to have the comfort and co-operation of so many of God's choicest saints. The fight in which the pilgrims are engaged needs the prayers and sympathy of the Lord's people, for the forces of evil are entrenched in human hearts and arrayed against Christian workers in many directions. Prayer Union members and friends have loyally stood with the workers in the place of prayer and generously supported them with their gifts. Many have helped practically with the moving of portable halls and caravans and in many other ways. Much is owed to those who are 'given to hospitality' and who show so much kindness to these itinerant preachers.

To all who lighten the pilgrims' burdens, cheer their hearts and encourage them in the work of the Lord, the pilgrim band, from its President to the youngest worker utters a hearty 'Thank you – God bless you' and means it! Without those who stand with the pilgrims, how could they operate? You who have given, you who have prayed, you who have been at times so inconvenienced, you who have gone just that extra mile and sacrificed your time and money – God bless you! God has seen it all and will reward you. It is not in vain that you have borne, together with those who are in the front-line of the battle, the burden and heat of the day. Do not despise the day of small things. A heart-warming word of encouragement here, a kindly action there, mean so much! And of course, keep praying! How the pilgrims need that more than anything else. Stand with them, and you will know too that your labour is not in vain in the Lord. 'As his part is that goeth down to the battle, so shall his part be that tarrieth by the stuff: they shall part alike' (I Sam. 30:24).

A comment from a paraphrased version should warm your hearts: 'Dear friend, you are doing a good work for God in taking care of the travelling teachers and missionaries who are passing through. They have told the church here of your friendship and your loving deeds. I am glad when you send them on their way with a generous gift. For they are travelling for the Lord, and take neither food, clothing, shelter, nor money from those who are not Christians, even though they have preached to them. So we ourselves should take care of them in order that we may become partners with them in the Lord's work'. (III John 5–8).

Another important development in the sixties was that of the youth work, known as the Young People's Fellowship. It had its beginning in a week-end houseparty in Edinburgh in July 1960, but it was inaugurated at Bangor Convention in 1963. Miss Isabel Story at the Edinburgh Headquarters meant a great deal to this aspect of the work. It developed quickly and spontaneously. It had its own badge and bi-monthly newsletter. Various house-parties at conventions and rallies were arranged with Mr H. Spain as Field Representative and Mr D. Howden as overall Director.

In 1964 it had a membership of 263, and of the fifty students at the College, eighteen were YPF members. In 1966 membership was over 400 and over thirty YPF members were in the Bible College.

By 1968 membership had risen to 600, and 130 of them were engaged in a Modified Bible Correspondence Course. In September that year Miss Story married and later with-drew from the work. At that time there were fourteen branches of the Youth Work each with its own committee, organizing its meetings and outreach programme. By 1970 the crowds of young people at the houseparty at the Bangor

Easter Convention had grown to 150, and in Edinburgh to 100. What a thrill to see so many young people at these major conventions.

As time went on the Districts themselves took over much of the organization of the youth activities and the structure of the work changed. Over the years weekend seminars, houseparties at conventions, youth camps and other activities have been arranged for the young people and these have been greatly blessed.

At the moment the work is thriving with a freshness and a vitality which is most encouraging. Bangor conventions of recent years have been memorable for the numbers of earnest and delightful young folk thronging the meetings.

One event which must not be overlooked during this period is the Mission's Eightieth Birthday when the whole Mission staff gathered together in Edinburgh in September 1966. It was a time of rich blessing and fellowship which spurred the workers on to yet greater heights.

Prior to this the whole Mission had gathered together on only four other occasions: in 1919, at the Bangor Convention; in 1936, the Jubilee year, at both Bangor and Edinburgh Conventions; and in 1946 at the Glenada Conference in Newcastle, Northern Ireland. During the Centenary year it is expected that the whole Mission will again attend both Bangor and Edinburgh Conventions.

CHAPTER 18

By All Means Save Some

Changing times and circumstances demand changed methods. The message is unaltered but the methods employed to transmit the message must of necessity change to meet prevailing conditions. It has been said that 'the price of progress is the willingness to change', but whatever changes are made must be made in the will of God.

Some of the major changes and developments in the seventies and eighties were the emergence of children's and youth camps and weekends, and the great expansion of the literature department of the work.

The basic method of campaigning in the villages has not been neglected but the sweeping victories of earlier days when communities were transformed by a mission held by two young lads or lassies have not been much in evidence lately.

Souls are plucked one by one in these hard villages. Here and there, there have been good breaks where numbers have sought God. Now and again pilgrims come into an area which has been well-prepared by the praying people of God, and a harvest is gathered. Christians are thrilled and encouraged then, of course, to see God moving in this special way. In Ireland we read of a mission where seventeen came to Christ for salvation. In Scotland over thirty trusted Christ in one mission, and at another seven were converted. Then five here and six there, and in a little isolated community another six professed conversion. And so they are reaped, here one or two and there three or four.

In one area in the Highlands the community was moved when nineteen were converted, and the results of this mission

The Mission's 80th Birthday Gathering in 1966

are still being felt. In these hard, unresponsive days, men and women come to Christ in a trickle whereas in former days they came in a flood.

'We never know what to expect when we go into the villages and housing estates and knock on the doors', says a pilgrim. 'Sometimes it's, "I'm not interested", or "shut yer face", or "I have my own church", or "tell me more", or – and how glad we are to hear this – "would you like to come in?" We've just got to be "Ready-for-Anything". At some doors no-one answers so through the letterbox goes a gospel tract and an invitation to the mission.'

The tenacity and dedication of these pilgrims as they refuse to give in to the hard conditions and as they intercede mightily on behalf of those who are not even conscious of their lost condition brings tears to many a Christian's eyes, and they glorify God in the lives of these fine young folk. There is an abandonment to Christ and a joy in service even as they go into the teeth of the battle. Despite the hardness, what joy it is when the light bursts into the lives of those for whom they have prayed.

The presence of God makes all the difference and gives the encouragement. It does not seem to matter so much when God is there. Of course, there is the deep regret that more do not come to hear the gospel, but how wonderful to know that He is with them as they work. 'There were only five in the meeting,' said the pilgrim, 'but that meeting stands out in my memory as one of the most outstanding times of the year. How our hearts were melted in His presence, and how easy it was to yield our all, afresh to Him. He came. That made all the difference'.

The ones and twos come to Christ, and they keep coming. 'A young Mormon woman found peace with God', runs a report. 'We had the privilege of pointing a lady of ninety to the Saviour', says another. 'Here at the seaside three teenagers trusted Christ for salvation'. 'A man who trusted Christ last year is being greatly used', says a pilgrim. 'A young couple saved when we last visited the village are growing by leaps and bounds,' joyfully exclaims another.

The gospel must get to the people and the pilgrims' ingenuity is taxed. A hundred years ago there were no caravan sites but now this affords a place for possible outreach. 'We have taken the gospel to the 750 caravans on this site', they said. 'We held two missions especially for the children', said a pilgrim.

In Eire a pilgrim spent a great deal of time visiting schools and convents with gospel films and Bibles and Christian literature. He reached literally thousands of young folk this way. Schools were found to be a fruitful avenue of communicating the gospel. 'It all depends on the headmaster', said one knowingly. 'He can open or close the door for you'. Fortunately they found a number of open doors, and in 1979, for instance, pilgrims in Scotland spoke to over 12,000 children in the schools at assemblies or in classes.

Other avenues were investigated. A barbeque drew over 200 people. Field meetings here and there were held, church-based missions were conducted, and of course, there are the villages – always the villages.

It is estimated that 12 million people live in the villages and rural areas of Britain. There are whole counties where no evangelist operates on a permanent basis to conduct missions. Millions of people of all ages, in our own country, are rushing to a Christless eternity, never having heard the gospel effectively.

In 1970, 2000 meetings were held by the pilgrims in Ireland alone with over 600 counselled during the year, 500 of these being first-time decisions. In 1975, however, in Ireland 512 were counselled, only 328 for salvation, and subsequent years have proved harder still. Scotland and England have both proved less responsive than Ireland.

The summer outdoor campaigns continue in several places each year. In the summer of 1984 there were thirteen Open Air campaigns. At Newcastle, N. Ireland, in 1978, there were at times over 400 listening to the gospel. Today it is almost as cheap to fly to Spain as to spend a holiday in other parts of the country, and off the people go. Even if they were in Newcastle the ease with which they move around today, does not guarantee an audience at the front. The car takes them where their fancy leads them, and that certainly is not to the preaching on the promenade. Numbers have decreased at the Open Air Campaigns but the witness goes steadily on with at times some striking conversions.

To reach the children, a camp was arranged in England. In 1974 another was begun at Cormeen, near Monaghan, Eire. 'Summer camps were a successful venture of our work last year', is the report in February 1975. The value of having children and young folk away for a week of teaching was enormous. Each day was crammed with activity catering for both physical and spiritual needs. Christian teenagers help with the camps and gain experience as well. There is always plenty of fun and happy activity. Young people soon get to know one another and often at the close of the camp when the parting time comes, they leave in a flood of tears. Their new-found Christian friends are left behind – 'but there's next year isn't there?!'

Camps are today a well-established part of Faith Mission ministry and in the summer of 1984 there were thirteen weeks of camps with 600 children attending, eighty of whom were led to Christ. In the summer of 1985 there were eighteen weeks of camps with more than 800 children attending, over 100 of whom trusted Christ for salvation. With more than three hours each day involved in biblical teaching and direct gospel communication, it certainly is a very worthwhile ministry, and one which many young people will never forget. Such concentrated teaching is absolutely essential in some areas where very little Christian truth is known.

Sometimes children's missions are held, like the one in Aberdeen in 1983, or the two-week mission in the Easter holidays at Fort William in 1985. Holiday time is especially useful as the children can be gathered in the mornings as well as in the evenings.

For the young people there are youth weekends, and house parties at most of the large conventions. Six weekends were arranged for the young people in 1985 in addition to the three 'School of Evangelism' weekends for young folk in the new centre in Ballymena.

Opportunities for summer service were offered as three of the Irish Superintendents took groups of young people to specific areas for happy fellowship and useful service in the front-line of evangelism in 1985.

All this shows definite progress in the realm of children and young people's work. This is a very demanding but happy and fruitful development, and one which has promise of increasing blessing and advance. With Mr Harry Spain as Youth Director, and the Superintendents and pilgrims doing their part, the youth work is moving forward in a way which, with God's blessing can bring new life and vitality to the work and indeed, to the country.

The seventies were difficult days in Ireland with death and destruction prevalent on every hand. 'There were two bomb scares this morning and we were hurried out on both occasions', said a pilgrim's hostess at the Bangor Convention. And she said it so casually half-way through a meal! The Scottish pilgrim gulped, but the hostess had become so conditioned to the troubles that she had not even bothered to mention it on her return from the town.

At times, however, there were long delays in getting to and from meetings because of actual bombs and also of bomb scares. Superintendents travel regularly over dangerous border areas and often late at night, but God has wonderfully preserved their lives and the lives of the pilgrims. In fact most of the superintendents drive over 20,000 miles a year in the interests of the work, and God has protected both them and the pilgrims in their many travels from accidents and death.

But the Mission did not go unscathed. On 17th July 1979,

Sylvia Crowe who had been in the Mission for five years, died instantly when caught in a bomb explosion. She was waiting at a bus-stop when it happened, and she became yet another victim of the tragedy of the troubles of Northern Ireland.

The ferocity of the bombing campaign has possibly reached its peak, and the troubles today are not as fierce as in the seventies. Travel is easier and the work of the Mission continues with very little restraint in all the areas of its operation.

CHAPTER 19

Advancing through Literature

The importance of reading and of the place of good literature in the life and experience of the Christian was recognized from the beginning of the work of the Faith Mission, and in 1888 the Christian Literature Co., came into being with a series of *Pilgrim Letters* issued monthly during that year. This was separate from the work of the Mission.

Then a small half-penny magazine called *Bright Words for Pilgrims Heavenwards* edited in England by the Rev C. G. Moore, a warm friend and supporter of the young Mission, was adopted in 1889 as the Mission's magazine, with a special Faith Mission edition, to which reference has been made in a previous chapter. The circulation increased splendidly and, the Scottish quickly outrivalling the English, the paper was soon taken over by the Mission entirely. In 1891 it was enlarged to the present page size which has been maintained ever since. In the course of the years other publications and reports were issued including a number of helpful books and booklets by the Chief, Horace Govan and others, some of which have been re-issued in more recent years and are still in circulation, but in the issue of *Bright Words* for June, 1912, the Chief made the following announcement:

> 'The Christian Literature Company now ceases as a separate concern, and the publishing of *Bright Words*, with the sale of it and any other literature, will be simply a part of the work of the Faith Mission.'

Office premises were obtained at that time at 262 Morrison Street in Edinburgh, which became the Mission's Headquarters and also housed the Publishing Department till 1952 when the nearby Govan House was purchased. An office and Bookroom in Belfast was secured in about 1923.

From these two small bookrooms the magazine was dispatched for many years, thousands of copies each month, to the Prayer Unions and other subscribers. The pilgrims were encouraged to have bookstalls on their missions; the books being supplied to them by the bookrooms. Apart from the larger cities there were few places where helpful Christian literature could be obtained, and Prayer Union members, and others also, in country places were only too glad to avail themselves of the services which the bookrooms in Edinburgh and Belfast offered. As the years passed these bookrooms became increasingly busy, and as far as Edinburgh was concerned the move to Govan House in 1952 gave the Mission more commodious and more suitable premises.

In 1925 the James Street Hall in the centre of Dunfermline was bequeathed to the Faith Mission which was then responsible for the services. Some years ago in premises adjacent to the hall, a small bookshop had been opened which created considerable interest in the town and neighbourhood and it was realized that it met a real need. Then came the news that a development plan had been devised for the town which would involve the demolition of the James Street Hall, for which the Mission would be compensated.

With the help of the money received in compensation the Faith Mission acquired a centrally situated property in Dunfermline which not only provided first-class accommodation for a bookshop, but where there was also a small hall available for the Prayer Union, and for conferences and similar gatherings.

A few years before, one of the pilgrims had expressed his concern for work with Christian literature, but the Mission had nothing to offer him at that time, with the result that he spent some years in Christian bookshops gaining experience of all that was involved in such work. The Council felt clearly led to offer him the post of Bookshop Manager in

Dunfermline, which came to him as a confirmation of God's leading as he was himself considering making application to return to the Mission. Accordingly in 1975, Mr Sandy Moynan came back to the Mission to take charge of the Scottish bookshops, and the spacious and beautiful property in Dunfermline became the centre for the Scottish literature work. God prospered the work which increasingly is meeting a real need in the area.

The shop in Peterhead had already been in existence for five years when the Dunfermline Centre was opened, and this has shown splendid growth. In fact in June 1985 another property was secured and the move to this was made. It serves the Christian public well and bears a bright witness in North-East Scotland.

In Stirling there was an interesting development. The Christian proprietor of a department store in the town offered the Faith Mission a site within his own shop for a literature centre, and in November 1982, the Faith Mission moved in.

In May 1985, the same thing happened in Berwick-on-Tweed, and now the Mission operates two of its shops within the precincts of large department stores. Paisley was another opening. In August 1983 this shop opened and God has set His seal to this move as well. The five Scottish shops are doing well and the Lord is blessing this aspect of His work. Ten years have passed since the Dunfermline centre was opened and the work has expanded enormously in this time.

If that could be said of Scotland how much more could it be said of Ireland. In 1972 Mr Edward Douglas, who had been in the Mission work for a number of years, was appointed as the Faith Mission bookshop manager in Ireland, where the work has developed out of all recognition. As the business grew it overflowed into other rooms in the building and at the moment that whole section of the building has been taken over as the headquarters of the Mission and the bookshop.

An enormous amount of literature is sold and all Ireland has felt the impact of the flood of Christian literature pouring into the country through this channel. Other bookshops were opened: Portadown was the first in January 1971, then Cookstown in 1975, Lurgan in 1977, Ballymena in 1981 with Bangor and the Clandeboye Shopping Centre in Bangor close on its heels, Lisburn in 1983 and Londonderry in 1985.

In Eire the 'Christian Literature Centre' which was operated for some time in the town of Monaghan was replaced by a spacious building in the centre of the town. The eight bookshops in the North and the one in the South have made a considerable contribution to the circulation of good Christian literature in the places where they operate. About sixty evening book-displays are held each year for the Irish churches, meeting a real need.

At the Christian Booksellers' Conference at Blackpool in 1982 the delegates voted the Faith Mission Bookshop in Belfast the 'best bookshop of the year' in Britain, and Mr Douglas was presented with the cup. He is at the moment the Chairman of the Christian Booksellers' Association of the United Kingdom.

Books can change lives, guide thoughts, shape beliefs and direct actions. There is no doubt that what we read makes an impact on our minds. Long ago Daniel Webster wrote: 'If God and His Word are not known and received, the devil and his work will gain the ascendancy; if the evangelical volume does not reach every hamlet, the pages of corrupt and licentious literature will'. Sadly his words were prophetic for today no country or town is without its 'licentious literature'.

How we need to be book enthusiasts! Even the best literature is worthless until it is read. How necessary to get books into the hands of those who need the message they convey. Books can be used in many, many situations, and with a little imaginative thinking, you are in business – the soul-saving business! Booklets, Scripture portions and books given prayerfully can bring eternal blessings. The sowing of a good book may reap the harvest of a transformed life, for books and booklets are effective instruments of evangelism.

Reference has already been made to the magazine *Bright Words* which became *Life Indeed* in January 1966. Except for a brief interlude, during the first seventy-nine years it had but two editors, Horace Govan and John Eberstein. When Mr Eberstein retired from the editorship in 1968, the Rev Kenneth Buchanan, the Principal of the Bible College was appointed Editor, which post he held till 1974, when Mr Andrew Woolsey became the Editor, having assisted Mr Buchanan at the College and with the editing for about three years.

Mr Woolsey was also responsible for writing the biography of the Rev Duncan Campbell, of which the late Dr Martyn Lloyd-Jones wrote that it was a 'carefully and judiciously written book'. It is a significant contribution to revival literature and is deservedly widely read being sold out in 1974, and reprinted in 1982 with the title 'Channel of Revival'. After a fruitful ministry in the Mission, Mr Woolsey withdrew in 1979 for further study and ministry.

Of the books which Duncan Campbell himself wrote, perhaps the best-known is, 'The Price and Power of Revival', for which there is still a continuing demand.

In January 1979, *Life Indeed* became a bi-monthly magazine. It was run by an editorial panel until January, 1984, when the present College Principal was appointed Editor. The July/August 1985 issue was No. 1120! Not many monthly magazines, either secular or religious, have produced over 1000 issues. *Life Indeed* has maintained a balanced spiritual tone and has been the link between the Mission and its many friends at home and abroad. It has consistently maintained its standard, its reading matter, its production and its reflection of the Mission as a living organism.

In 1938, with the fiftieth volume of *Bright Words*, 15,000 per month were published. It continued to be printed through the war years despite the rationing of paper. In fact in 1944, 18,500 were printed for the summer months and in 1948 the summer figures topped the 20,000 mark. The magazine survived the war in a remarkable way, and proved to be a source of inspiration and blessing throughout this tragic period. Today almost 10,000 are distributed bi-monthly with an increase in the summer months to 12,000.

The magazine takes its honoured place in the world of Christian literature, and should God be pleased to continue to use the Faith Mission as an effective instrument, the little magazine will continue to have a place in the hearts of those who have been touched by its ministry, and who appreciate its message.

Letters and notes sometimes with *Life Indeed* subscriptions, often encourage those working behind the scenes when they realise that time and again an article, a poem, a testimony or some paragraph has meant something very special to the reader, or that someone, somewhere in that wide-spread readership has yielded to the Saviour through the ministry of the magazine.

CHAPTER 20

A Living Vision for a New Era

One of the far-reaching developments of the seventies is that of 'area work', where married couples are placed in an area for a number of years. In certain areas there is so much ignorance of the Bible and indifference to the claims of Christ that more than the usual methods of evangelism are required. Instead of the normal three to six week mission, they would evangelize a given area for a period of years.

In 1976 Mr and Mrs W. Wright joined the Mission and they were placed in Oakham. Mr and Mrs N. Wilkinson were later placed in Hertfordshire. By 1979 there were three couples in England and one in Scotland. One of these workers in the Midlands of England visited about fifty villages over a period of five years in the late seventies and early eighties. He said, 'I knocked on almost every door, and I would estimate that, 1½% of the people are interested in religion.'

Times have changed. Such disinterest was unknown a century ago, and the work today has pressures of which the early pilgrims knew nothing. 'It's not like that in our area though', said another, 'for the people are willing to speak about the things of God'. It varies from place to place and the pilgrim must be 100% flexible in his methods.

With the aim of getting to know the people in their areas the workers use various methods. Literature has been widely successful as a means of contact. 'In over 4000 homes visited only 20 people have refused to accept free literature,' said Mr Wright.

It takes times to win the confidence of the people who would not normally be at all interested in gospel meetings; it

124

takes time to establish a relationship, but living in a community gives the opportunity of getting to know the folk and becoming a real friend to them. 'Always available', might be the area worker's motto, and people in the village know that should they come for help in a time of crisis, or telephone for counsel, they will not be disappointed. 'Pop over for a cup of coffee one morning', she would say, and Mrs Area Worker would wheel her pram with its precious contents to another young mother down the road. Of course babies are an endless source of interest, and stories are exchanged with a lot of mutual advice. Does that not give the opportunity to speak of another birth – a spiritual one?

Christmas is a time of great opportunity and workers are able to capitalize on the smiles and goodwill that abound. A little present here, a bunch of flowers there; it all helps to create friendship and confidence, and it all leads to those vital conversations which, when the interest is aroused, go on sometimes, well into the night. There is an aim, a purpose, a goal before them. They are called to lead men and women to Christ. 'Oh Lord, open the doors for an effective conversation where You can speak to his heart. Oh Lord, save him!'

The homely informality of the area work is carried into children's clubs, prayer meetings and fellowship conducted in homes or some centre which make such gatherings more attractive to people who would not ordinarily attend church services or mission halls.

The well-known voice of the minister came clearly over the phone, 'Can you take a service for me?' Yes, he could, and did; and that ministry is repeated in churches of various denominations with which the area workers co-operate, meeting the needs of the whole community.

Each area is unique, calling for special forms of outreach suited to the needs and character of the people. Some specialize in children's work, others in home Bible studies. Initiative, adaptability and wisdom are prime qualities necessary to fit the worker for the task. He might be called to help with a car repair, or to take someone to the doctor. Interruptions are part of his day's work – but he has an end in view! He is charged with the great message of God's salvation, and by all means these people must receive it.

At the moment there are six areas worked by couples, two in England, one in Scotland and three in Ireland. The full potential of this venture has not yet been reached, but this is most certainly a method which is meeting a need and finding great acceptance.

'Nine people were in the "Neighbours' Meeting" last week and one lady was visibly moved by the truths explained to them', said one. 'After most of the folk had gone', said another, 'we sat in the kitchen till 2 a.m. I had no idea of her great need, but at last she is beginning to see the light of God'. 'It's going to take some time with this dear couple because of their total ignorance', said a third sadly. But, praise God, there comes the time when the Spirit applies the Word savingly to their hearts, and the joybells ring!

With the approach of the Centenary and conscious that God's spirit was moving in the Mission, the leaders of the Faith Mission met for four days of prayer and discussion over the New Year period of 1984 at the College in Ravelston Park, Edinburgh. 'The greatness of the need, and the lateness of the hour, and the wide open doors before us all added to our responsibility to seek God and His plan for the future. We realized that the aims of the Mission were unchanged and the Commission of the Lord was still to "Go and tell" but our concern was to know how best to fulfil those aims. We were confident that the Lord was leading us to trust Him for something new, and His voice was clearly saying to us "Go Forward". We felt therefore that we dare not "mark time". We must go forward and set definite goals for the work'. So writes Mr Percival, the General Director. The goals were clearly set out:

'To open at least six new centres for area workers during the next five years and at the same time increase the numbers of workers for our missions in the villages.

To reach out to new areas hitherto untouched by the Mission's ministry. For some time the areas of Cornwall and Devon have been prayerfully considered for missions and it is now planned to move workers into this area.

With this new sense of thrust and expansion we reaffirmed the Mission's policy to place additional superintendents as the work develops.

To endeavour to obtain larger premises to meet the increasing needs of our Bible College and also provide facilities for a Convention Centre.

To maintain the present devotional and soul-winning emphasis in training at the Bible College but also to expand the course to enable students who would appreciate the opportunity of gaining a recognised qualification, such as the Diploma in theology, to do so.

To explore and develop video and tape ministry to give a wider field of ministry to our Bible College and Conventions'.

This 'Edinburgh Manifesto' reveals a sense of urgency and expectancy, of faith and courage, of joy and hope, of commission and purpose, of the great possibilities and the urgent necessity for men and women to join forces with us as we move forward together. It is a battle-cry. It is an indication of trust in a great God who has not failed in 100 years nor is likely to do so now. It closes with:

'We firmly believe God is calling us to move into a new era in the work of the Mission and that He will wonderfully meet the need for personnel, housing and equipment to reach these goals'.

Council members left those meetings with a song in their hearts. God was giving new vision and breathing new life into the work.

The secularized and materialistic society with its increasing permissiveness and scepticism and its growing obsession with the occult is still there. But the call of God has come and in impossible situations possibilities are seen. God is giving a fresh vision of Himself and of what He can do in spite of human failure and sin. Men of faith are needed just now; men who live where they can see the invisible and touch the intangible, where they will do and dare for God. May the Mission respond to the call and realize its God-given potential as by faith it possesses its possessions:

> Doubt sees the obstacle,
>   Faith sees the way,
> Doubt sees the darksome night,
>   Faith sees the day,
> Doubt dreads to take a step,
>   Faith soars on high,
> Doubt whispers, 'Who believes?'
>   Faith answers 'I'.

'In the last three years', said an influential Christian at the Easter Bangor Convention in 1985, 'there has been a turn. God is with us'. Others sense it too. Who could forget that Tuesday morning at Bangor in 1983 when the Spirit of God swept through the congregation and scores of young people and older ones too, bent in brokenness in God's presence?

'We had a great Youth Weekend at Kilkeel this year', comes the report in 1981. 'The Stornoway Convention has been the best since the days of the revival', says the Superintendent in 1983. 'The children's and teenage camps is an expanding and fruitful ministry', says the Youth Director.

In summing up part of the year's work the General Director said in May 1984: 'We can truly praise the Lord that mercy drops have been falling. We have been very conscious of the

128

Lord's hand upon the many activities of the mission and especially upon the convention ministry. Some of the convention reports that reach us say that they were "the best for many years".

At Bangor many responded in the meetings and there was a great sense of God's presence'. In January 1985, he could say, 'The Lord has been at work in a very wonderful way'.

Cornwall and Devon were part of the vision, and into Cornwall and Devon they went. Two lady pilgrims did the early work and gained a great deal of goodwill and acceptance. At the end of summer in 1984 Mr and Mrs Wilkinson were appointed to the area. They are there now and the work in this area is gaining ground and experiencing God's blessing.

In Co Cork, the Christian friends united their efforts, and in a very generous way, a spacious bungalow was built for the area workers at Bandon, Mr and Mrs Stevenson. This is developing as a camp site, and children's camps are held here with great appreciation and blessing. Portable halls donated to the Mission were conveyed to Bandon and erected there. In the same way another bungalow was provided for the Mission in the Irish Midlands, and Mr and Mrs Wilson now occupy this beautiful new property. Both these homes were donated in 1984. The new Stradbally Convention in the Midlands of Eire is another great encouragement.

Large portable halls were given to the Mission in 1984 and these were transferred to the Faith Mission property on the outskirts of Portadown and erected for use as a convention centre. This is a tremendous step forward in Ireland and provides facilities for children's camps and youth activities. The youth fellowship which meets here regularly is thriving, and Mr T. Matthews the Superintendent, is very encouraged.

In 1927 the Faith Mission acquired a church in Ballymena and this has been used down the years for conferences and

Prayer Union gatherings. The present superintendent in Ballymena, Mr John Bennett, saw possibilities in the building. A floor was put in half-way up the walls creating a two-story building with rooms built in the upper section. An ablution block was added together with a kitchen and dining hall, and a convention centre with sleeping accommodation for up to 80 young people was created. It has already been put to excellent use. The practical help and gifts of interested friends have been a wonderful encouragement.

True, missions are hard, dreadfully hard at times, but the pilgrims plod bravely on looking to the Lord who has sent them, who equips them, and who uses them to lead men and women to the Saviour. At present the Mission numbers more than eighty workers plus the more than thirty-two bookshop workers. This number is strengthened each summer by the Bible College students working with the pilgrims on their campaigns.

A backward glance over the century would show that an outstanding characteristic of the Faith Mission has been its permanence. The President, Mr Eberstein once wrote:

'It is true that there have been missions which have proved fruitless, but on the whole, the words that could be written as descriptive of the work of both past and present are: "Fruit that remains". All over the country there are those who have been brought to Christ through the labours of the pilgrims, some of whom are exercising a ministry of no mean importance. Others are witnessing quietly and consistently by holy, consecrated lives, and little is known of them outside their immediate neighbourhood. There are also people who meet regularly for united prayer in larger or smaller groups which owe their beginnings to the work of the Mission.'

The danger of growing old is of dwelling in the past and not pressing on in the power of the Spirit to new attainments. Many a work begun in the Spirit has developed along stereotyped lines, with resultant loss of vision, lack of vitality and leakage of power. God help the Faith Mission to have a willingness to obey Him should He indicate the need for change, a flexibility to implement the change, a freshness and openness of spirit toward God, and a clarity of purpose toward man in the task which is committed to its hand.

Having come to the centenary the Faith Mission is certainly not existing merely to preserve itself. Light is shining on the pathway and faith is kindling in the heart. Possibilities are opening up before it. The primary object which brought it into being, that of bringing men and women to Christ, is thankfully still its primary object and we trust that it will ever remain so.

CHAPTER 21

The Fruitful Bough

When the dying Jacob blessed his sons he said that Joseph was 'a fruitful bough by a well, whose branches ran over the wall' (Gen 49:22). Never in his wildest dreams could that young Glasgow businessman J. G. Govan, have estimated the worldwide effects of the decision that day on the island of Arran when he sat on the rocks and gazed at the ships. What a moment of destiny. How much hung on his choice whether to spend his life in prosperous ease or to give himself utterly to Christ to carry the gospel into the neglected villages of Scotland.

Thousands upon thousands have been swept into the kingdom in this country. Those who could never have thought it possible to enter Christian service have had opportunity to do so, and having gained experience in God's work, have gone into other spheres where they have been greatly used by God. Many men of great calibre who have become leaders in many areas of God's work were either led to Christ by the pilgrims or influenced for Christ by their ministry. There are ministers in nearly all the denominations who look back gratefully to their early days with the Faith Mission. There are missionaries in the far-flung corners of the earth, some of them former pilgrims, working with numerous societies who date their first strivings Godwards, their sanctified walk with God, or their call to Christian service, to their association with the Faith Mission.

More specifically however there are three societies which sprang directly from the Faith Mission and which perpetuate the same methods and message in their spheres of service.

The first of these is the Africa Evangelistic Band in

Southern Africa. The three distinguished ladies, May, Emma and Helena Garratt from Blackrock, Eire, who were so greatly used, particularily in Donegal, sold their beautiful home and went to South Africa in 1916. This again was a momentous decision but many in Southern Africa thank God today for the effects of the work of the AEB in their own lives and communities.

From South Africa they wrote to Mr Govan asking him to send a District Superintendent to begin the work there. He replied that as God had led them there He evidently meant them to begin it themselves. They gathered a Council together and founded the AEB in 1924. The first few South African workers were trained in Edinburgh until a Bible College called 'Glenvar', after their home in Blackrock, was established in Cape Town.

Pilgrim work as they had known it in this country was established in South Africa with the pilgrims doing the same itinerant work as they do in Britain. It has spread all over South Africa, South West Africa (Namibia), and in the earlier days Rhodesia, now Zimbabwe. There are District Headquarters, Convention Centres and two Bible Colleges with pilgrims working amongst all classes and colours.

The work amongst the so-called Coloured peoples of South Africa, whose language is either Afrikaans or English, has prospered greatly and there is a team of Coloured pilgrims operating with much blessing.

The AEB entered into the Black townships of the land until this developed to the extent that in 1945 it became a separate Mission and has maintained a great witness in these areas over the years. For a time the AEB had missionary work in Botswana, and its work in Zaire was well established with several mission stations manned by twenty-six workers at the time of the enforced evacuation in 1960. Since then this work has been taken over by neighbouring societies and still continues.

One of the AEB workers felt called to form a youth mission

amongst the Black communities in South Africa and this continues to be a witness today. Another two went to Japan, each eventually forming a different society there, both of which are respected and strong movements today. The AEB itself has about 110 workers in all and continues to make an impact across the country.

The rural areas of South Africa are largely Afrikaans speaking, so the work, which has majored on the country districts, has become to a large extent Afrikaans. God has greatly blessed the AEB down the years and many, many lives have been transformed through contact with the pilgrims and their burning message of salvation through faith in Christ alone.

All this because long ago a young man made the choice to give his life to God for His service as he looked at the ships gliding along on the water below him. All this because three cultured ladies gave up their beautiful home and exchanged it for an unknown land which needed the gospel. What destinies hang on decisions in the will of God!

The second society is the Faith Mission in Canada. On the day that John George Govan was buried, in September, 1927, two pilgrims, Helen Gibb and Phebe Rowdon sailed for Canada to begin the Faith Mission work there. Other lady pilgrims joined them and in less than two years over 700 meetings had been conducted.

In 1929 a Canadian Advisory Council was set up, at the first meeting of which the need of a man as a District Superinten- dent was stressed. The following year Mr John Eberstein arrived to superintend the work and stayed for two years before returning to Britain. In 1933 Mr J. Allan Wallace, a young man with several years of pilgrim experience in Britain, came to superintend the work. In 1946 the house which had been used as the Mission headquarters was sold and a suitable property was purchased in Toronto to serve as Headquarters.

In the early days goodly numbers of adults were converted

from year to year, but with the passing of time openings for evangelistic services were more difficult to find. In later years the emphasis has been placed on youth work and children's work, for the simple reason that adults do not readily attend interdenominational evangelistic services. On the other hand, there is a response amongst the children.

In the first fifty years of the work in Canada, up to 1977, some 3000 missions were worked in various parts of the country. These include evangelistic campaigns, Daily Vacation Bible Schools, beach campaigns and youth missions. During the past six years, invitations to conduct Daily Vacation Bible Schools in churches have greatly increased in Ontario. In the summer of 1985 thirty-seven DVBS were conducted in churches in Ontario, in which some 850 children were reached. Open air work has been extended and this continues each summer, particularly in British Columbia.

The Faith Mission began in Ontario, and in 1941 opened up across the continent in British Columbia when Mr and Mrs W. MacFarlane established a headquarters in Vancouver. In 1951 Mr and Mrs K. Buchanan opened up Nova Scotia and established a headquarters in Oxford. In the early sixties the work in the Maritimes was closed because of a lack of workers. The Faith Mission works now almost exclusively in Ontario and British Columbia, with a little work being done in Quebec as well.

Since 1969, *Faith Mission Men*, groups of men who unite to help the Mission in practical ways, has been a real source of encouragement to the pilgrims.

Mr and Mrs Wallace retired from the Mission's directorship in 1979 after leading the work for forty-six years and contributing greatly to its advance.

During 1984 over 153 gospel meetings were held, 21,000 children attended special meetings and DVBS with about 250 being counselled for salvation. The thirteen Canadian pilgrims under the directorship of Mr Hugh Jamieson continue to press on with the work of evangelism in this vast country.

The third society is the Faith Mission in France or Mission-Foi-Evangile. In 1928 a young Swiss Christian arrived at the Faith Mission Training Home in Edinburgh. There and in the practical work, Ernest Aebi learned many lessons, and put them to good use as a well-known Scripture Union evangelist in France and Switzerland, and later as Principal of the Emmaus Bible School in Lausanne. After the war, when a long-time French friend asked him where his sons should best train for evangelism, without hesitation he referred them to his own experience.

So it was that in 1947 Jean-Paul Krémer, one of those sons, went to train in the Faith Mission, followed in 1948 by his brother Stephen, and in 1951 by his sister Lydia, and later by several other young people from France and Switzerland. A number of them were already thinking of working for the Lord in the spiritually dark land of France where little pioneer Christian work was being done, and nothing at all in the towns and villages of Central France.

When in 1960 the Mission-Foi-Evangile was actually begun in Central France, most of the workers had years of training behind them in the Faith Mission, and the new work was largely based on that training and experience. Of course there were adjustments to make and new methods to work out that could be better adapted to the French culture. The philosophical and religious history of France all render its population largely impervious to the gospel, to a degree not seen even in the most difficult parts of the British Isles; even its material setting makes evangelistic work more difficult.

The Mission in France has grown and changed over the years. Caravans and portable halls have at present been largely set aside because of official requirements. The necessity of founding permanent evangelical churches where none existed is another (foreseen) development of Mission-Foi-Evangile, while retaining its non-denominational character.

As is to be expected in a predominantly Roman Catholic

country they have had to face difficulties and opposition, despite which however, God has blessed the work and many have been brought to Christ. Today there are about sixteen workers operating in teams and contributing much to the vital Christian witness in the country.

As we look at the spreading branches of the fruitful bough we can exclaim, 'what God hath done!' Who can tell how great the results will be when but one young person yields fully to God. From those prayer meetings in Water Street, Glasgow, in 1885, there flowed a stream which grew into a mighty river sweeping many into its glorious tide of blessing.

The Church in Scotland, England and Ireland has been immeasurably enriched. The Church in Africa, Canada, France, Japan has known seasons of refreshing from the presence of the Lord through the instrumentality of societies which sprang from the same root. Many will rise up in that day and praise God for raising up these movements which brought them the good news of God's great salvation.

THE BIBLE COLLEGE
18 Ravelston Park, Edinburgh

CHAPTER 22

Preparing for the Battle

As early as 1890 the Chief was feeling the need for a central Training Home and Home of Rest, but it was several years later that training was actually commenced. The pressing needs of the work drew the young people into it without adequate training or preparation which was not ideal or satisfactory.

Finally a property was purchased in Rothesay called 'Mount Clare', which for part of the year was let to missionaries and other Christians, thus reducing the cost of the upkeep and the training sessions. A special fund for training purposes was opened. Training commenced in 1897, the course lasting three months. Several of these courses were held but they were irregular, and the special fund was soon exhausted.

In 1910 Mount Clare was sold as it had involved considerable financial expense and was not fulfilling the purpose for which it was originally intended.

The vision of an effective training programme for the Faith Mission and the work of God everywhere burned in the heart of the Chief. It had never left him, and now it became a priority. Not just three months, but nine months in the Training Home and three months in active evangelism must constitute the training.

A property was rented in Joppa Park, Portobello, on the outskirts of Edinburgh. The first session began in October 1912, closing in June 1913. There were six men and women in residence for the first term, nine for the second, and eleven for the third. Five of those trained in the first session were candidates for the South African mission-field who would first of all do a short term in the Faith Mission.

God greatly blessed that first training session. At one half night of prayer the Spirit of God visited the little band of students, and for days the students could do nothing but pray. The Spirit of the Lord pervaded the place. Lectures were put aside as students met with God in prayer. The heart of the work had been touched, by God. The effect of this was felt throughout the Mission. Confidence was restored, and with it new hope for the future. Somehow the Spirit surged through all parts of the work. Donations began to increase, and there was a sense that the tide was rising.

Then something happened which set the Mission completely on its feet. A letter was received with a gift of £2,500 from a wealthy shipowner in Glasgow, Mr J. P. Maclay (later to become Sir Joseph Maclay, and in 1922 Lord Maclay, having been Shipping Controller in the First World War). He had long been an admirer of the Chief and his work. He wrote: 'I trust that you will kindly accept this gift. The value of your personal work together with the Faith Mission workers is so great that I appreciate it a privilege so to help'.

It was with this gift that Rosemount (as it was then called) in Ravelston Park was purchased. For more than seventy years it has been the place where pilgrims have received their training and from which streams of spiritual blessing have flowed through the hundreds who studied there. There have been some outstanding times of blessing when the Lord has worked powerfully through the power of the Holy Spirit. One such was in the ninth session when an invitation was received to undertake an evangelistic mission from the Training Home from the Superintendent of the Carrubbers Close Mission.

As the proposal for a mission in the City during training was rather out of the usual line of work it required considerable time for prayer and thought, but the Chief wrote: 'We came to the conclusion that it was of God'. The mission went on for nine weeks – much longer than had originally been intended, interfering to some extent with the studies of the students, but the practical experience gained was invaluable.

The Chief wrote further: 'A great deal of visiting was done and the students were given a great welcome to the houses, and it was wonderful how ready the people seemed to be for spiritual conversation . . . we were out of ruts too in the speaking. There were no long addresses. Usually two or three addresses each evening, and testimony occupied a more important place than preaching. It told too . . . large numbers responded, some seeking for the first time to yield themselves to the Lord Jesus Christ for pardon and eternal life, and others through full surrender to prove the fullness of salvation. We do not put much stress on figures in spiritual work'. It was evidently a time of outstanding blessing and was often referred to as such in the years that followed.

Many applications were being received for training, more than it was possible to accommodate, and at this time there are frequent references to this in the Chief's notes in *Bright Words*, such as 'the question of possible increased accommodation for training was discussed and was to be made a matter of prayer'. Again, 'The fact of our having more suitable candidates than we can accommodate, and more openings than we can undertake with our present staff, seems to point to the urgency of more room. We want to be sure of the Lord's leading and to have His guidance as to whether we should enlarge Rosemount, or get an additional house.'

Prior to the eleventh session he wrote: 'It will not be possible to have a large house for the coming session, but if sleeping accommodation can be had somewhere not far from Ravelston Park we may be able to accept a few more'. The needed accommodation was secured and he wrote: 'This has been our largest session. We had twenty-three students and, I think, our busiest and our best'.

In 1925 an additional house was purchased at 5 Queensferry Terrace, but in 1927 came the sudden Home-call of the Chief.

After his passing Mrs Govan took over his responsibility as

far as the Training Home was concerned with Miss Rosie Govan as her helper. The question of the needed accommodation, however, was ever present and it was agreed to build an extension to 18 Ravelston Park, the cost of which was met by a further generous gift from Lord Maclay.

While the work of the new building was in progress of construction Mrs Govan was stricken with a fatal illness, but she had the satisfaction of seeing the completion of the extension before she passed away on July 26, 1932.

On her mother's death Miss Govan continued to be in charge with the able assistance of Miss Ellen Tickner as Matron, and Mr P. S. Bristow in charge of the men students. She continued for six years, when she felt called to the work in South Africa to join Miss Helena Garratt, the sole survivor of the three Garratt sisters, who had been responsible to a large extent on the human level for the opening up of the work in Ireland.

At the Perth Convention in 1937, one of the speakers was Mr D. W. Lambert, who had for many years been assistant to the late Dr Samuel Chadwick at Cliff College. He spoke with much acceptance and sometime afterwards wrote to Mr J. A. A. Wallace, the President of the Mission, with an enquiry as to whether there was a place for him in the ranks of the Mission.

Coming as it did at the time that Miss Govan had intimated that she had heard God's call to South Africa the Council felt quite clearly that he should be invited to become Principal of the Training Home. Of this appointment the President wrote: 'We feel confident that we have been led to the man of God's choice in the person of Mr D. W. Lambert, MA, of Cliff College, where he has been greatly used of God'. Mr and Mrs Lambert came to Edinburgh in January 1939. Then came the War with the problems it created. Mr Lambert's period at the Training Home was fraught with difficulties, shortage of students and a variety of other things consequent upon the War. It was during his time that the period of training was extended to two years, and that the Training Home was renamed 'The Training Home and Bible College'. It was at this time also in 1944 that the house at 1 Ravelston Dykes was purchased to replace 5 Queensferry Terrace to house the men students, and later to provide a lecture room. The strain of the war years, however, had told upon him and his wife, and in 1946 he and Mrs Lambert resigned, after almost eight years of dedicated and devoted service, having left his mark on those who trained under him to which many willingly bore testimony. They felt God was leading them to a new field of service in Berwick-on-Tweed.

On Mr Lambert's retiral Mr Eberstein, then Director of the Mission, but resident in Glasgow, came to Edinburgh and was given charge of the College with Miss Tickner as Matron, now free to return to the work, having been freed from the responsibilities which led to her retiral. She died, however, in 1949, her place as Matron being taken the following year by Miss Helen Kirkwood, who continued as such till her retiral in 1971.

From time to time there have been remarkable times of blessing at the College – one such being in 1925, when the Chief was in Switzerland for a period and Mrs Govan was in charge. There was at this time a real visitation of the Spirit. In 1956 there was another such, when the Spirit of God came amongst the students in an unusual way. 'Two characteristics were outstanding: there was a spirit of love shed abroad – the sense of unity had to be experienced to be believed – and the spirit of gladness was very evident. Love and joy are after all the first two manifestations of the Spirit. Those of us who had the privilege of sharing in the blessing of those days are never likely to forget them!'

In 1958 Mr Eberstein, as President of the Mission, took Mr Bristow's place at Headquarters and the Rev Duncan Campbell was appointed Principal of the Bible College where he remained for nine years. His time there was truly owned of God and it left a very evident mark on the students. He was much in demand for engagements outside of the College, and there is no doubt that he had many a heart-ache in coming to a decision about which calls he could accept, and the friends he was obliged to disappoint. He was held in high esteem in Christian circles all over the country, which had a considerable impact on the College and the Mission as a whole.

His retiral was a serious matter and it was most important that the right man be appointed to succeed him. He himself had a part to play in this. On one of his visits to Canada he had met the Rev Kenneth Buchanan, who at that time was a lecturer at the Prairie Bible Institute after having worked in the Faith Mission in Canada for fourteen years. Contact was made with him and in August 1967, Mr and Mrs Buchanan came to Edinburgh, the former taking up his responsibilities as Principal of the Bible College and taking over the editorship of *Life Indeed* the following year.

After ten years of service as Principal of the College Mr Buchanan felt the time had come to return to Canada with his family. He was a man of prayer, and successive generations of students have much appreciated his lectures and devotional ministry at the College.

The Rev Arthur Neil from Swansea, who had pastored several Baptist churches in England and Wales accepted the invitation to become Principal and began in September 1977. His preaching and teaching at the College were highly valued, but after two years he felt led to withdraw from the Mission.

Mr David Howden was then appointed to this important post. He was deeply spiritual and had given many years of outstanding service to the Mission, first of all as a pilgrim conducting missions, then as a District Superintendent, and later as Director for England, when the development of the work in Yorkshire and the Midlands owed much to his leadership and guidance. All this was to be of great value to him in this new responsibility, but tragically on the 28th of November, 1981, he suddenly passed away. A booklet was later produced about his life and service, 'A Vessel unto

Honour', a fitting tribute to one who was so devoted. Mr Dale accepted the responsibility for the two remaining terms of the session.

The Mission Council then felt led to invite the Rev Colin Peckham, Principal of the Bible College of the Africa Evangelistic Band in Cape Town, to the position, and in July 1982, he with his wife, formerly Pilgrim Mary Morrison, and family, arrived in Edinburgh to begin the new session in October. The College continues under his leadership at the moment.

A total of sixty students took the three-month courses which were held at Rothesay many years ago. Apart from these, by 1936, the Jubilee Year, which was the twenty-fourth session since moving to Edinburgh, 430 students had been trained, 'the majority of whom are still engaged in Christian work', ran the report. The Mission's seventy-seventh year, 1963, was the fiftieth year of the work in East Anglia as well as of the Bible College in Edinburgh. In those fifty years, 850 young people completed the course. From 1964 to 1985 a further 437 students have been trained (192 men and 245 women) making a total of 1287 during the seventy-two years of College work in Edinburgh, which is an average of eighteen students per year. It is at the moment stretched to its full capacity with forty-nine students, and it is hoped, in accordance with the expressed desire of the Council, soon 'to obtain larger premises to meet the increasing needs of the Bible College'.

CHAPTER 23

The Bible College Today

'Those tense moments at the breakfast table when on occasions your name is called and everyone is waiting for you to repeat the day's memory verse – oh, will I ever forget it!' Then he smiled, 'but how wonderful to have those verses at my fingertips now. I don't know how I could handle an open-air meeting without having such a store of vital Scriptures which so often just pop up as I speak.' He is not the only one who has realized that memorizing the Scripture in College pays rich dividends. Students are taken through the different themes of important doctrines and learn verses from each section until at the end of the two-year course they look back in amazement at over 300 verses which they have mastered. 'I just couldn't do it,' they had said at first, 'but it is done!' One by one those verses were conquered. Tenaciously they kept at it and their lives have been marvellously enriched ever since. To quote Scripture is to speak with authority. Nothing equips the soul-winner more effectively than memorized Scripture.

The Bible is, as everyone would expect of a Bible College, central to the course. Quite apart from all the other studies, each student must read the Bible through twice during the two-year course to familiarize themselves with the stories, themes and teachings of this Book of books.

Young people coming to the College are soon launched into the lecturing programme. It starts at 9.30 most mornings and four lectures follow before dinner, the afternoons and evenings normally being devoted to study. How privileged the College has been down the years to have such able and spiritual Bible teachers grace the lecture room. Evangelical

146

ministers from churches in and around Edinburgh have given their time and abilities so willingly. They come from various denominations but they all hold to the essential doctrines of the faith believing without question that the Bible is the Word of God. From their busy lives elsewhere they come and expound not only the great doctrines of the faith, but they bring rich practical experience to the classroom as well.

Who can fail to marvel as the panorama of redemption unfolds in the sweep of Bible Survey. Most of the New Testament books are examined in a more detailed study, together with a number from the Old Testament. Biblical doctrines form another main section of the study course. The doctrines of God, of Jesus Christ, of the Holy Spirit, Man, Sin, Salvation and others, form a body of truth which is essential for every Christian worker to know.

To this main biblial thrust other subjects are added to make up a full-orbed Bible College course. Take, for example, the subject of Homiletics. Why, who ever will forget Homiletics? Certainly not those who rose to preach their trial sermon in the lecture room! English classes are given for those who need them.

Church History unearths the very distant beginnings of the Church and figures like Polycarp and Constantine fall into place. Over the centuries the students stride to the mighty Reformation when Luther stood before the Diet of Worms and cried, 'Here I stand.'

Then there is the subject of Evangelism and Personal Soul-winning, lectures on Children's Work, Modern Cults and other subjects, which all combine to give a very satisfactory and well-balanced College course. Visiting speakers from the Mission and from other societies as well, bring freshness and blessing, broadening the students' vision to the range of possibilities and scope in the Lord's work everywhere.

The atmosphere in the lecture-room is constantly changing from laughter at times, to awe as the great doctrines of the

Faith are expounded; from wonder as 'gems' of scriptural truth are discovered, to joy as light falls on some intricate passage of the Word. What rare illumination comes in these lectures – flashes of spiritual light! Sometimes the presence of God is such that a lecturer stops and allows one and another to pray. The teaching has awakened new desires, new purposes, new resolves. Each lecture is taped for later study as required, and some lectures are videoed for a wider teaching ministry.

Each term some spiritual classic is prescribed for students to read. Some who have not been used to reading much have discovered for the first time the value of literature, and their appetites are whetted to read more. Each term an assignment is required as well. It could be the travels of Paul, the geography of Palestine, the doctrine of justification, or prayer, or faith. As they delve into the volumes in the library and look into the meanings of Scripture, they appreciate more and more the privilege of opening their minds and hearts to biblical instruction and spiritual revelation.

A very necessary aspect of training is that of the outreach programme. Students in teams engage in different activities each week. 'Pub' visitation is at times difficult as they speak to people who have little thought of God. Students help local churches with their door-to-door visitation.

On the Mound in Princes Street they hold a weekly open-air meeting on Sunday afternoons, weather permitting. Tracts are distributed, and students preach, sing and testify or speak to passers-by, some of whom have sought the Lord. Invitations constantly come to the College from various churches or fellowship groups for students to come and minister, and the scope of these opportunities is varied and useful. Sometimes they follow up a contact made at some meeting or outreach programme with blessed results. One such incident happened in a local hospital when a student led a twelve-year-old girl to the Lord. On her return, the lady in the next bed exclaimed that she had heard the conversation and she too wanted to come to Christ. The student led her to the Lord and heard later that day that the lady had passed away only two hours after she had received Christ!

The finest practical experience comes, of course, when they are allocated to the different teams of pilgrims in various parts of the country in the summer. The summer work affords great opportunities, and during the summer of 1984 over 160 people were led to Christ at camps and campaigns. The students share in this spiritual harvest and mature remarkably by being so completely involved.

The most important aspect of all is that of getting to know God. There is a decided devotional emphasis at the College. What a tragedy it would be if students were to leave with their heads full of theology, yet with their hearts empty of divine love. Their minds must be saturated with biblical truth and doctrine and their hearts filled with evangelical passion. Not only must they get to know the Word of God, but the God of the Word as well. They must be thoroughly equipped to meet the demands of the day, and at the completion of their training must leave the College as flames of fire ready to blaze a mighty trail for God.

With this chief end in view times are set aside daily for students to wait on God. Morning and evening devotions are held in their rooms at their bedsides, while morning prayers are conducted together after breakfast each day. The College family all meet every Friday morning for a two-and-a-half hour prayer meeting. What an oasis these prayer meetings have been. Praying is inspired as the presence of God so often breaks through amongst the students. Prayers ascend, some in brokenness, all in earnestness to the One who hears and answers. This prayer meeting is the heart of the College, and it is to this that many former students refer in later years as the outstanding feature of their training. Sometimes dinner has to be delayed as students and staff find fullness of joy in the hush and glory of His gracious presence. After one such delay the principal apologized to

149

the staff for upsetting their well-prepared meal. 'That's nothing at all,' they exclaimed, 'we just wish that we could have been in on the blessing too!'

In the midst of the busy programme characters are being formed. Living together with folk from many different backgrounds and outlooks develops tolerance, acceptance and appreciation of another's viewpoint. Being shaped by God is an adventure of faith and obedience. 'Through lectures, prayer times and life in general among my fellow students, I found that I was not the person I thought I was. God has been re-shaping me,' said one. 'Precious lessons have been learned,' said another. 'The balanced programme of Bible teaching, spiritual guidance and practical training gave me the best possible grounding. It enabled me to surrender completely to Christ and experience the fullness of God's blessing in my life,' said one who is now a minister of a church in Scotland.

Every year there is an Open Day when the members of staff and students mingle with the numbers of interested friends who are conducted around the buildings in groups. There is the display of assignments and other items of interest and a selection of slides illustrating the many aspects of College life. Many remark on the warm and friendly atmosphere of the College and feel that they are visiting a 'family home'. 'There is an atmosphere here,' many a visitor has said, 'I have been so conscious of the peace and presence of the Lord Himself.'

Like the Mission as a whole, the College is a massive faith venture, for the students' fees meet only a portion of the expenses of the College. The rest comes from the Christian public in gifts large and small. No gift is too insignificant and all are gratefully acknowledged and placed directly into Christian work. Without these contributions from God's people the Mission and the College just could not function.

The range of student ability and former education is quite wide, for some come to the College not having had the benefit of an extensive education, while there are normally teachers, nursing sisters and a university degree or two among the group. All however, have one thing in common, a desire to meet with God at College and a willingness to apply themselves to the course of study. This they do with a will, knowing that what they learn will be of enormous benefit when they enter Christian service.

Arriving at the College is a great moment for new students. Some have battled with the call of God and have eventually come to the conclusion that the only thing that they can do is to go in obedience to the call of God. So many questions have had to be settled. 'Would I have enough money to pay the College fees? What will my parents say? How will my friends react? Would I be able to understand the lectures? How would I respond to the spiritual challenge of the course? And the preaching? How could I preach? But the call has been plain, personal and persistent. I can neither avoid nor escape it. How solemn to sense that the mighty God is calling and commissioning me. The call is not something that I can regard lightly for the awful judgement of God rests on those who must hear the gospel through my lips.

God is sovereign in His choice of and purpose for His messenger. He sends whom He will, where He will, and His call is His enabling. As I follow, the plan unfolds. I am no longer my own and must follow the Master's directions. Impressions have come to my heart and they have become convictions.

This call does not depend upon my abilities, nor do they necessarily determine my sphere of service. I am in the hands of God, and I turn from ambitions and prospects. I would not be diverted from His purposes by the lure of the lesser loyalties. Position and friendships I put on the altar. If God has marriage for me, I will welcome it, but it must be in His will. I embrace God's will for my life. I am His forever, and am His responsibility as I go in His strength. I abandon myself to Him and know that He will lead me in victory and joy to accomplish His purpose and to fulfil His desires for and through me. It does not matter how inadequate or unsuitable I feel, He will lead me. Moses felt inadequate didn't he? And so did Gideon and Jeremiah, but God was able to use them.

With Isaiah I say, "Here am I Lord, send me." The Spirit constrains me, the Scriptures confirm His call to me, the circumstances surrounding me convince me that I must move out at His command, the call of human need everywhere confronts me with a sense of responsibility and conviction that I should go, and Christ's command cannot be evaded. He has said "Go" and I must obey.

'O Lord, I present myself to You – my will, my time, my talents, my tongue, my property, my reputation, my entire being, to be and to do anything You require of me. Now, as I have given myself away, I am no longer my own, but all the Lord's. I believe that You accept the offering I bring. I trust You to work in me all the good pleasure of Your will. I am willing to receive what You give, to lack what You withhold, to relinquish what You take, to suffer what You ordain, to be what You require, to do what You command, to go where You send, to wait till You say "Go".'

These great moments of consecration have come to some, and others will still have to face them, but the students arrive, fresh and eager to fulfil the call and the will of God. Perhaps young people reading this will respond as so many have before them, to yield fully to the Saviour and to trust Him with their whole future. How wonderful the call of God is – precious, real, humbling, glorious. Paul said that he was 'separated unto the gospel' (Rom 1:1). This surely is undeserved in grace and unparalleled in glory.

CHAPTER 24

Go Forward!

In the Coronation service the monarch is presented with a Bible by the Archbishop who says that this Book is 'the most valuable thing that this world affords.' It is well-known that Queen Victoria attributed the greatness of Britain to the prominence given to the Bible in the life of the nation. At the tercentenary of the Authorized Version King George V said, 'It is my confident hope that my subjects may never cease to cherish their noble inheritance in the English Bible.' King George VI said, 'I recommend the reading of this Book. For centuries the Bible has been a wholesome and strengthening influence in our nation's life, and it behoves us in these momentous days to turn with renewed faith to this divine source of comfort and inspiration.'

But the Bible, this Book that changes lives, alters communities, uproots cultures, transforms nations, has ceased to be a major factor in the life of the British nation. Churches once brimming over with vibrant life and joy, where the preaching of the word of God once thrilled the overflowing congregations, stand solemn and empty, a condemnation on the wide-spread spiritual apostacy today. According to the telling 1984 census of the churches conducted by the National Bible Society of Scotland, 17% of the adult population of Scotland attend church every week. This compares favourably with 9% in England, and 13% in Wales. Of course many of these folk are in the upper age bracket, and the church and the Bible have generally ceased to be a factor to be reckoned with among the younger generation.

In these modern days people of many nationalities have immigrated to this country, and they have brought their

THE FAITH MISSION COUNCIL *January 1986*

Back Row: T. Matthews, E. Douglas, J. Bennett, A. Morrison, A. Moynan, V. Harper.
Middle Row: Rev. J. Finlay, R. Dukelow, S. Hay, Rev. W. Smylie, D. Metcalfe, H. Spain, D. Bennett,
Rev. C. Peckham.
Front Row: S. Clarke, J. McNeilly, J. Blanshard, Rev. T. Shaw (president), K. Percival, W. Porter, A. Dale.
Absentees: Misses M. Dawson, I. Cummings, J. Watters and V. Carson.

religions with them. Schools have been forced to modify their religious instruction programmes, and instead of teaching the Scriptures, many schools teach comparative religions. The Bible is wrenched from the hands of the young. They have no reason to want to go to church, for their parents are not particularly interested and there are many attractions beckoning them on Sundays. If the local minister is not evangelical the service is not inspiring and of course does not draw them. That means that they do not receive biblical teaching in either the school, which so often has withdrawn the biblical syllabus, or the church which they do not attend. They don't get the Bible! They have no clue about biblical history or teaching. They would not know whether Moses was among the twelve apostles, or whether Abraham was the son of Simon Peter, if indeed Abraham was a biblical character at all. Tragically, during the last fifteen years the Bible has ceased to be the bedrock of national life, and consequently evil can only multiply. The moral principles derived from the Bible, which made this nation great, are no longer authoritative or binding simply because as a whole they are not known. Consciences are seared, and disorder and crime increase on every hand. The changeable views of politicians and national leaders are the poor substitutes for biblical guidance. Who is right anyway? Every man does that which is right in his own eyes.

Fortunately this is not the norm in Northern Ireland, but it is to a large extent in Scotland, and more so, and in an increasing measure, in England. The housing estates are in many instances simply pagan communities. Children have no instruction in biblical matters and must be taught the very, very basic things about God. Pilgrims returning from these areas are simply shattered by the total ignorance of the children and young people. Many come from Christian backgrounds with biblical teaching and cannot conceive that in this country such ignorance can exist. It is like going to the mission field. England is a mission field! A mission field that desperately needs the morality and standards of the Bible once again to be clearly proclaimed and uncompromisingly preached. It needs the message of Christ's love and mighty delivering power. It needs to be called back to a faith that once made it great. It needs the Bible! It needs young people who will be willing to go and bring its message to them.

More than all of that it needs a great outpouring of the mighty Holy Spirit which will sweep evil before it in sanctifying power and will turn men and women back to God. Without such a move of the Spirit it is inevitable that Britain will move towards becoming a totalitarian state. Authority must be found, and if it is not found in God it will be found in a dictational system of bondage and of God-rejecting atheistic communism. There is no time to play at religion. There is no time to utter pious platitudes of meaningless jargon. The people have long since turned a deaf ear to all this. They need reality. They need God.

It is against this backdrop that the pilgrims of 1986 are working, and must take stock of themselves and of their progress. In the face of the desperate need the work of the Mission is absolutely essential, for men and women are dying in ignorance and sin. If the Mission were to become merely a monument to the glorious achievements in the past, to the glowing records written in the pages of history the sooner it is buried the better. A monument is to something in the past. It is a dead thing. God save the Mission from ever becoming that. It must be a movement motivated by divine inspiration, by the mighty power of God. It must be a living organism, and not become a dead organization. It must have the vision of a loving Saviour who looked on the needy crowds and had compassion. It must have the passion of a suffering Saviour who did not count the cost in His awesome mission to save mankind. It must have the action of an obedient Son who knew his Father's will and did it. The Spirit of the Christ must totally possess each member of the Mission as they launch into the ministry to which they are called. All must be ready to march forward in spite of hard resistance or cold indifference, in spite of obstacles or stumbling-blocks, and continue to fulfil the purpose for which the Mission was brought into being.

The gaze of the Mission's leadership and of each member and prayer-partner must be fixed on God-given goals. Conscious of these special objectives, and, pulsating with life and expectancy, they must seek to implement them in the power of the Holy Spirit. Is God not the same today as yesterday? He said to Moses, 'Certainly I will be with thee' (Ex. 3:2). To Joshua he said, 'Have not I commanded thee? Be strong and of a good courage; be not afraid, neither be thou dismayed; for the Lord thy God is with thee withersoever thou goest' (Joshua 1:9). 'In the Lord put I my trust,' said the Psalmist (Ps 11:1). As the old era was slipping away and the news was about to dawn, the dying king David charged Solomon his son saying, 'be thou strong . . . and keep the charge of the Lord thy God' (I Kings 2:2,3). Azariah the prophet said to Asa the king as well as to all Judah and Benjamin, 'The Lord is with you, while ye be with Him . . . be ye strong therefore, and let not your hands be weak: for your work shall be rewarded' (II Chron 15:2,7). When Haggai was encouraging the people who had returned from captivity to build again the house of the Lord, he said, 'Be strong, all ye people . . . and work: for I am with you, saith the Lord' (Hag. 2:4). To the Corinthians, to the Ephesians, to Timothy, Paul cried out, 'Be strong'. At the birth of the Faith Mission God's clear word was, 'Have faith in God,' and 'Seek first the Kingdom'. This is still God's Word to the Mission today.

The new century is dawning, and God who provided so miraculously for the Mission with all its needs throughout the last century is still the same today. His promises still hold good. He is still Jehovah-Jireh, the Lord who provides. He is still the glorious Conqueror, still able to bare His mighty arm and reveal Himself as the God of battles, the God of revival.

Shall we not trust Him to lead us on in triumph into the next century, to reveal Himself in the future as He has done in the past, to be uplifted in the Mission and in the midst of His rejoicing people as He sweeps to victory in one town and village after another. 'If God be for us, who can be against us?' (Rom. 8:31).

Such dedication and service inevitably costs, but if the right calibre of worker is found in this next century, the price for advance will be paid, and the Mission will press forward into victory. In fact, it stands poised for this advance right now. The demand is upon the spiritual life of the worker. When General Booth was asked the secret of his success, he said, 'God has had all there was of me to have. There have been men of greater opportunities; but from the day I got the poor of London on my heart, and a vision of what Jesus Christ could do, I made up my mind that God would have all of William Booth there was.' That is the kind of dedication the Mission wants, needs and must have of all its workers if any vital impression is to be made on Britain in the next century. It can afford nothing else.

John Knox said long ago, 'Give me Scotland or I die!' That kind of passion must possess and control the Faith Mission in order that it might move forward in triumph. It must be sold out to God, it must have a single eye to God's glory, it must 'seek first the Kingdom of God,' it must know its God and then do exploits. John Wesley expressed his desires for a dedicated people in the following words, 'Oh that God would give me the things which I long for; that I may see a people wholly devoted to God, crucified to the world, and the world crucified to them; a people truly given to God in body, soul and substance.' Let the pilgrims lead the way! Let them prove by their consecrated lives that their work is worthy of the prayers and support of God's people. Let them take courage as they hear God say, 'Be strong for I am with you!' Let them go forward in total dedication of all that they have and are, in complete obedience to the One who knows the end from the beginning and whose reasons for any commands are founded in His great omniscience, in a spirit of prayer and glorious expectancy, in faith in a great God, ready to shoulder responsibilities and prepared to work hard, let them go forward conquering and to conquer.

Would it not be wonderful if God were to crown these living offerings with the evident tokens of His mercy in the revelation of His power? How the pilgrims would rejoice to breathe the atmosphere of heaven should God come and visit His people once again. How precious would be another outpouring of divine favour. Oh Lord send us revival! Long ago Horace Govan wrote these telling words:

> Visit us Lord with revival,
> Stricken with coldness and death,
> Where is our hope of survival
> Save in they life-giving breath?
>
> Surely 'tis time for revival,
> Surely soon dawneth the day;
> Soon shall we hail its arrival
> Chasing the shadows away.

His burden for revival was expressed in his own bold, graphic and unique way, as Rev W. P. Nicholson of Ireland said:

> 'God is still waiting to be enquired of by us for a real heaven-sent revival, in which men fall at the feet of sovereign mercy and pray for themselves, and weep and mourn so much that critics would almost think that they have gone insane; a revival that will make the preachers forget their manuscripts and burst out weeping in the pulpits; a cyclone of mysterious omnipresence, which when it strikes a church or community, will make people awfully mad or wonderfully happy.
>
> 'Nothing is so alarming as the utter absence of alarm in our churches. Nothing is so awful in my mind as that sinners have no terror of sin or the judgement. Oh, that God would so baptize with fire a thousand people as to render them

incomprehensible amazements of power! Oh, for a few men so dead to all things but God, and so filled with Him, as to make them more than a match for the rest of mankind!

'Oh, Thou Triune God of Sinai, Calvary, and Pentecost, art thou not nursing under the horizon, the lightning and thunder and rain of an amazing sweeping world-wide revival? Let it come, Lord! Let it come soon! Let it strike our nation even though it hurl our abominable church pride in the dust, thrust all our philanthropic fairs and festivals into the gutter, blow the French music out of our choirs, confound all the wise, and be understood by no one but by Thy divine self. Thou art master of Thine own tempests. Oh, send us a storm of Holy Ghost power and fire before Thou sendest the storms of Thy judgements upon us!

'Why will not the preachers, churches and assemblies of our land unite in waiting on God in united prayer and intercession, with fastings and confession of our lack before the Lord, until He sends us a mighty Baptism of Pentecostal revival fire, with a burning passion for lost souls, so that as God's Zion travaileth, thousands will be born again and their names written in Heaven? Oh, for such a revival, world-wide, to the glory of God alone!'

If God were to send this sweeping through the land, the pilgrims would be the first to rejoice and to give the glory to Him. Until such time they will watch and wait, work and pray, and gather men and women into His kingdom for His glory.

How good is the God we adore,
Our faithful, unchangeable friend,
Whose love is as great as His power
And knows neither measure nor end!

'Tis Jesus the First and the Last
Whose Spirit shall guide us safe home:
We'll praise Him for all that is past
And trust Him for all that's to come.

To God be the glory!

The Lewis Awakening
1949–1953

by
Rev Duncan Campbell

Revival has always captivated the interest of the workers of the Faith Mission. A number had seen the movings of the Spirit in many places. Duncan Campbell who came from the Western Highlands entered the Faith Mission in October 1919, and was destined to be greatly used in this realm. He continued in the Faith Mission until his health compelled him to take up work not entailing nightly preaching. He gave twenty-five years to the United Free Church, and then, because of the clear leading of God and his great concern for the Gaelic-speaking people in the Highlands and Islands of Scotland, after a year of prayerful consideration, he rejoined the Mission in January 1949. To Skye he went, and during a succession of missions there, he saw a good response, but it was in the Isle-of-Lewis where he was to see God move in a remarkable way.

Lewis and Harris together form an island west of the most northerly part of Scotland, eighty miles in length, with a population of some 25,000 people. Stornoway is the only large town. Although there are lonely places, most of the folk not in Stornoway live in more or less compact villages. In several places these villages are so near to each other as to constitute a large community within the compass of a few miles. The people are largely occupied in crofting and weaving on looms in their own houses and it is here that the famous Harris tweed is produced. Gaelic is spoken all over the island. The people are instinctively and traditionally religious, with the old-time reverence for God, His

Word and the ordinances of the church.

From the praying people of Barvas and their parish minister, came the request that Mr Campbell go to Lewis for a series of meetings. In December 1949, he went; and he was certainly 'a man sent from God'.

'The Lewis Awakening 1949–1953' written by Rev Duncan Campbell after the movement, is reproduced in the following pages:

The Need of Awakening. The island of Lewis has been the scene of a very gracious movement of the Spirit. The breath of revival has been felt, and communities have been conscious of the mighty impact of God. This island had, in days past, experienced seasons of refreshing from the presence of the Lord, but of late years the stream of vital Christianity appeared to be running low. This view was shared by the Free Church Presbytery of Lewis who, in the following declaration, publicly expressed their deep concern: 'The Presbytery of Lewis having taken into consideration the low state of vital religion within their own bounds, and throughout the land generally, call upon their faithful people in all their congregations to take a serious view of the present dispensation of divine displeasure manifested, not only in the chaotic conditions of international politics and morality, but also, and especially, in the lack of spiritual power from gospel ordinances, and to realize that these things plainly indicate that the Most High has a controversy with the nation. They note especially the growing carelessness toward Sabbath observance and public worship, the light regard of solemn vows and obligations so that the sacraments of the church – especially that of baptism – tend to become in too many cases an offence to God rather than a means of grace to the recipients, and the spreading abroad of the spirit of pleasure which has taken such a hold of the younger generation that all regard for anything higher appears with very few exceptions to have been utterly dismissed from their thoughts.

'The Presbytery affectionately plead with their people –

especially with the youth of the church – to take these matters to heart and to make serious inquiry as to what must be the end, should there be no repentance; and they call upon every individual as before God to examine his or her life in the light of that responsibility which pertains to us all, that haply, in the divine mercy, we may be visited with the spirit of repentance and may turn again unto the Lord whom we have so grieved with our iniquities and waywardness. Especially would they warn their young people of the devil's man-traps – the cinema and the public-house.'

The foregoing is an extract from a Free Church Presbyterial declaration, as published in the Stornoway Gazette and West Coast Advertiser (December 9th, 1949).

The decline referred to in this declaration began to show itself in a growing disregard for the things of God; indeed the blighting influences of the spirit of the age, with its deadening effect, was so effective that in certain parishes very few young people attended public worship: the dance, the picture-show and the 'drinking-house'* were institutions which could now thrive in Lewis, on the generous support given by their willing devotees.

True, Lewis has its traditions. The time-honoured practice of family worship is still observed in most homes. The great doctrines of the Christian faith, such as the total depravity of man, justification by faith on the ground of Christ's atonement, regeneration by the Spirit, and the sovereignity of God in the affairs of men are central in the theology of Lewis. But then it is possible to have a name to live and yet be dead, and has not experience demonstrated again and again that man can be orthodox in sentiment yet loose in practice? Correct views of Scripture do not constitute righteousness.

What effect the foregoing declaration had on the Christian church in Lewis is beyond the knowledge of the writer, but it

* Not a public house, but a small house or bothy in which men gather regularly to consume drink which they have purchased elsewhere. At the time the only licensed premises in Lewis were those in Stornoway.

is certain that most would regard its publication as timely, and its contents a true representation of the situation.

Lewis, however, was not devoid of a virile Christian witness. In all denominations men could be found who were true watchmen on the walls of Zion, and who longed for the day when the desert would again 'rejoice and blossom as the rose'. In most pulpits throughout the island, the evangel was proclaimed with passionate personal conviction, and not infrequently, in certain congregations at least, signs followed the preaching of the Word. The weekly prayer meeting was still a vital part of its religious life, although in too many cases attended only by a faithful few. But the Most High did not despise the day of small things: and Lewis was soon to see the mighty power of God let loose in a gracious outpouring of His Spirit and it came

> 'As dew upon the tender herb,
>   Diffusing fragrance round;
> As showers that usher in the spring,
>   And cheer the thirsty ground.'

How it began. In his book, The Second Evangelical Awakening, Dr Edwin Orr, referring to the American Awakening of 1858, writes: 'A divine influence seemed to pervade the land and men's hearts were strangely warmed by a power that was outpoured in unusual ways'. Every genuine revival of religion has known the gracious touch of God's mighty power falling from on high, moving men as no other power can move them to seek after God. 'Oh . . . , that Thou wouldest come down, that the mountains might flow down at Thy presence' (Is 64:1), was the cry of the prophet of old. Was Isaiah conscious of the futility of man's best endeavours? Had he come to the end of all human resources? It appears so. This is the place to which the praying group in the Parish of Barvas in Lewis came, and it was this consciousness and conviction that, throwing them upon the sure promise of God, gave birth to the Lewis Revival.

In writing of the movement, I would like first to state what I mean by revival as witnessed in the Hebrides. I do not mean a time of religious entertainment, with crowds gathering to enjoy an evening of bright gospel singing; I do not mean sensational or spectacular advertising – in a God-sent revival you do not need to spend money on advertising. I do not mean high-pressure methods to get men to an enquiry room – in revival every service is an enquiry room; the road and hillside become sacred spots to many when the winds of God blow. Revival is a going of God among His people, and an awareness of God laying hold of the community. Here we see the difference between a successful campaign and revival; in the former we may see many brought to a saving knowledge of the truth, and the church or mission experience a time of quickening, but so far as the town or district is concerned no real change is visible; the world goes on its way and the dance and picture-shows are still crowded; but in revival the fear of God lays hold upon the community, moving men and women, who until then had no concern for spiritual things, to seek after God.

To the praying men and women of Barvas, four things were made clear, and to them became governing principles. First, they themselves must be rightly related to God, and in this connection the reading of Psalm 24 at one of their prayer meetings brought them down in the presence of the Lord, where hearts were searched and vows renewed, and, in the words of one who was present, they gave to their lives the propulsion of a sacred vow, and with Hezekiah of old, found it in their hearts to 'make a covenant with the Lord God of Israel'. Happy the church and favoured the congregation that can produce such men and women! So prayer meetings were held in church and cottage, and frequently the small hours of the morning found the parish minister and his faithful few pleading the promises, with a consciousness of God, and with a confidence in Him that caused them to hope in His Word.

In the second place, they were possessed of the conviction

that God, being a covenant-keeping God, must keep His covenant engagements. Had He not promised to 'pour water upon him that is thirsty, and floods upon the dry ground'? Here was something that for them existed in the field of possibility; why were they not actually experiencing it? But they came at length to the place where, with one of old, they could cry 'Our God . . . is able . . . and He will'.

> 'Faith, mighty faith the promise sees
>   And looks to God alone,
> Laughs at impossibilities
>   And cries "it shall be done".'

Thirdly, they must be prepared for God to work in His own way and not according to their programme – God was sovereign and must act according to His sovereign purpose – but ever keeping in mind that, while God is sovereign in the affairs of men, His sovereignity does not relieve men of responsibility. 'God is the God of revival but man is the human agent through whom revival is possible.'

Fourthly, there must be a manifestation of God, demonstrating the reality of the divine in operation, when men would be forced to say, 'This is the Lord's doing, and it is marvellous in our eyes'. It is therefore not surprising that in the month of December, 1949, God did visit the Parish Church of Barvas with revival blessing that, in a very short time, leapt the bounds of the parish, bringing refreshing and spiritual life to many all over the island.

Here mention must be made of the part played by the parish minister, the late Rev James Murray MacKay. For months he and his office-bearers had prayed for an outpouring of the Spirit of God, and now the time had come when they felt that, as a congregation, they were called upon to act. But so wonderful are the ways of God that the minister of Barvas had to go to Strathpeffer Convention to have revealed to him through the ministry of the Rev Dr T. Fitch, now of Belfast, the action to be taken: Great was his encouragement on returning to his parish to be told that God, in a vision of the night, had revealed to one of the praying group not only that revival was coming, but also the instrument to be used as a channel; the person revealed in the vision was the one mentioned at Strathpeffer! 'In a vision of the night, when deep sleep falleth upon men, in slumberings upon the bed; then He openeth the ears of men, and sealeth their instruction' (Job 33:15,16). So it was that word was sent to the director of the Faith Mission in Edinburgh, as a result of which I found myself in Lewis in December, 1949.

The supernatural working of God the Holy Spirit in revival power is something that no man can fully describe, and it would be folly to attempt it. There are, however, features of the Lewis revival which also characterized revivals of the past, one of which is the spirit of expectancy. Here I found a group of men who seemed to be living on the high plane of implicit confidence in God. That was the conviction and assurance that breathed in every prayer offered in that memorable first meeting of my sojourn in the Hebrides, and my first contact with this congregation fully convinced me that revival had already come; it was to be my privilege to have some small share in it. One will never forget the hush of the awful presence of God as we sat waiting for the opening Psalm to be announced; truly one could say:

'And Heaven came down our souls to greet,
And glory crowned the mercy seat.'

Here is a scene witnessed during the first days of the movement: a crowded church, the service is over: the congregation, reluctant to disperse, stand outside the church in a silence that is tense. Suddenly a cry is heard within: a young man, burdened for the souls of his fellow men, is pouring out his soul in intercession. He prays until he falls into a trance and lies prostrate on the floor of the church. But heaven had heard, and the congregation, moved by a power that they could not resist, came back into the church, and a wave of conviction of sin swept over the gathering, moving strong men to cry to God for mercy. This service continued until the small hours of the morning, but so great was the distress and so deep the hunger which gripped men and women, that they refused to go home, and already were assembling in another part of the parish. An interesting and amazing feature of this early morning visitation, was the number who made their way to the church, moved by a power they had not experienced before: others were deeply convicted of their sin and crying for mercy, in their homes, before ever coming near the church.

None of those present will forget that morning meeting as the assembled company sang:

'I will not come within my house,
   Nor rest in bed at all;
Nor shall mine eyes take any sleep,
   Nor eyelids slumber shall;

'Till for the Lord a place I find,
   Where He may make abode;
A place of habitation
   For Jacob's mighty God.'

There was a moving scene, some weeping in sorrow and distress, others, with joy and love filling their hearts, falling upon their knees, conscious only of the presence and power of God who had come in revival blessing. Within a matter of days the whole parish was in the grip of a spiritual awakening. Churches became crowded, with services continuing until three o'clock in the morning. Work was largely put aside, as young and old were made to face eternal realities. Soon the fire of blessing spread to the neighbouring parishes. Carloway witnessed a gracious manifestation of the power of God that will surely live in the annals of Lewis revivals. The minister of that parish was assisting with the meetings at Barvas: God was mightily at work, and a number of men were in great distress of soul. Two of these were pipers who were to have played at a concert and dance at Carloway. The minister of Carloway had had a concern to witness at this dance. Leaving the meetings at Barvas, he arrived at the dance at about 3.30 a.m. Almost immediately after he entered the hall the dancing ceased, and he thereupon proposed that they should sing two verses of a Gaelic Psalm. Not all were immediately favourable to this, but after a special appeal Psalm 139, verse 7, was sung, some present joining in:

> 'From Thy Spirit whither shall I go?
>   Or from Thy Presence fly?
> Ascend I Heaven, lo, Thou art there;
>   There, if in Hell I lie.'

He then engaged in prayer and followed with a few words of exhortation, and suddenly the power of God swept through the company and, almost immediately, the music of the dance gave place to the cry of the penitent. Opposition broke down under conviction of sin and distress of soul. This applies especially to a schoolmaster's son who was acting MC. Before leaving the hall the minister related the news that the pipers and others who were to have been at the dance had decided for Christ in the kitchen meeting at Barvas two hours before. Soon the whole proceedings came to an end and those present dispersed to their homes bewildered and amazed. That same night, in his own home, the schoolmaster came under deep conviction and the following Monday his wife also completely broke down. They then blazed a trail for God in their parish, and Ness became the scene of a most gracious movement.

At Ness meetings were held in the afternoon and evening, and frequently on into the morning. Churches, halls, private houses, and even furniture and meal stores were used to accommodate men and women seeking for God.

Perhaps the greatest miracle of all was in the village of Arnol. Here, indifference to the things of God held the field and a good deal of opposition was experienced but prayer, the mighty weapon of the revival, was resorted to and an evening given to waiting upon God. Before midnight God came down, the mountains flowed down at His presence, and a wave of revival swept the village: opposition and spiritual death fled before the presence of the Lord of life. Here was demonstrated the power of prevailing prayer, and that nothing lies beyond the reach of prayer except that which lies outside the will of God. There are those in Arnol today who will bear witness to the fact that, while a brother prayed, the very house shook. I could only stand in silence as wave after wave of divine power swept through the house, and in a matter of minutes following this heaven-sent visitation, men and women were on their faces in distress of soul. It is true that in this village God had His 'watchmen'. Thank God there are many such in Lewis and Harris; it is one of such who, when he witnessed the mighty power of God in this village, asked that we might sing the 126th Psalm:

'When Zion's bondage God turned back,
   As men that dreamed were we,
Then filled with laughter was our mouth,
   Our tongue with melody.'

Some time ago, while passing through this village, I was met by an old man whose salutation was in the following words, 'I am glad to be alive to witness this day'. Then, pointing to a particular house, he said, 'Do you see that house? That was the "drinking house" of this village, where our young men met in utter disregard of God, His Word, or His day. Today it is closed and the men who frequented it are praying in our prayer meetings'. What a joy it is now to see such numbers going to the house of God on the Sabbath, or looking forward with joyful anticipation to the weekly prayer meetings. Some time ago I remarked to a friend: 'That is surely a wonderful sight', referring to the large numbers of people going to church. 'Yes', he replied, 'but before the revival one seldom saw more than four from this village going to church on Sabbath morning'. One young man, speaking for the youth of the district said, 'We did not know what church going meant until the revival came, now the prayer meeting is the weekly attraction, and the worship of God in His house on the Sabbath our chief delight'.

The spread of the Movement. The movement that began in the Parish Church of Barvas, almost immediately spread to the neighbouring Parish of Ness, and it soon became evident that it was not to be confined to these two parishes. From north, south, east and west the people came in buses, vans, cars and lorries, to witness the mighty movings of God and then to return to their respective parishes to bear testimony to the fact that they had met with the Saviour. A gamekeeper, whose home was twenty-four miles from Barvas, was so wrought upon and burdened for the souls of others, that his van was seldom off the road and for two years, night after night, brought its load of men and women who were seeking for Jesus. He was rewarded by seeing many coming to the Saviour, including members of his own family. It is therefore not surprising that in the Parish of Lochs, where the gentleman referred to had his home, a gracious movement should break out. Here the ground was well prepared by a faithful ministry, and great was the rejoicing when sower and reaper saw the fruit of their labour in a harvest of precious souls. As in Barvas, meetings here continued until two and three o'clock in the morning and some remarkable scenes were witnessed as the Spirit of God moved among the people.

An incident occurred in this parish which is still vivid in my mind. A lorry was engaged to convey a number of people to a meeting: the distance to be covered was about fourteen miles, and the journey would take them round the end of a loch. Unfortunately, the lorry broke down when they were about seven miles from their destination. The younger of the party decided to walk, but this was too much for the older members who, very reluctantly, retraced their steps homeward. Suddenly it occurred to them that a late meeting would be held, and if they could secure a boat they could cross the loch and be in time for the midnight service. A boat was found at the nearest township three miles distant, and on rowing across the loch, a distance of three miles, great was their satisfaction to find a meeting in progress; and was it the guidance of the Spirit that led the preacher that night to take as his text, 'They also took shipping and came to Capernaum, seeking for Jesus'? The men from across the loch were seeking for Jesus, and that night they found Him. That morning, just as the dawn was breaking and night gave way to the rising sun, another Sun had arisen, and One of clearer shining brought light and life to men who sat in darkness. Before they set sail for home, the congregation gathered and, led by one of the local ministers, sang:

> 'When all Thy mercies, O my God!
>   My rising souls surveys,
> Transported with the view, I'm lost
>   In wonder, love, and praise.
>
> 'Oh, how shall words with equal warmth,
>   The gratitude declare
> That glows within my ravish'd heart!
>   But Thou canst read it there.
>
> 'When nature fails, and day and night
>   Divide Thy works no more,
> My ever-grateful heart, O Lord,
>   Thy mercy shall adore.
>
> 'Through all eternity to Thee
>   A joyful song I'll raise,
> For, oh! eternity's too short
>   To utter all Thy praise.'

It is not often that strangers from other districts crowd a church, making it impossible for the regular congregation to get accommodation in their own building, but this actually happened in this parish. So great was the hunger for the Gospel that, long before the hour of service, buses and vans from a neighbouring parish brought a crowd that filled the little church of Habost, and the regular congregation were content to sit in the vehicles that the strangers had vacated. 'This is the Lord's doing, and it is marvellous in our eyes.'

The influence of the Lewis awakening was felt in Harris. Soon in both Tarbert and Leverburgh a gracious movement broke out, and one interesting feature of this blessed visitation was the place that singing had in the meetings. Again and again a wave of deep conviction of sin would sweep over the congregation, and men and women would be seen bending before the mighty impact of the Spirit, as the heart-cry of the penitent found expression in the words of Psalm 130:

> 'Lord, from the depths to Thee I cry'd.
>   My voice, Lord, do Thou hear:
> Unto my supplication's voice
>   Given an attentive ear.

> 'Lord, who shall stand, if Thou, O Lord,
>   Should'st mark iniquity?
> But yet with Thee forgiveness is,
>   That fear'd Thou mayest be.'

Bernera is a small island off the coast of Harris, with a population of about 400. In April, 1952, it was my privilege to visit this parish and witness one of the most remarkable movements of the revival. Here, as in other districts, there were men who, on their faces before God, cried for an outpouring of His Spirit; and an incident occurred which goes to demonstrate the power of prevailing prayer and to reveal how true it is that 'the secret of the Lord is with them that fear Him'. One morning an elder of the Church of Scotland was greatly exercised in spirit, as he thought of the state of the church and the growing carelessness toward Sabbath observance and public worship. While waiting upon God, this good man was strangely moved, and was enabled to pray the prayer of faith and lay hold upon the promise, 'I will be as the dew unto Israel'. This word from God came with such conviction and power, that he was assured that revival was going to sweep the island, and in that confidence he rose from his knees.

While this man was praying in his barn, I myself, taking part in the Faith Mission Convention at Bangor in Northern Ireland, was suddenly arrested by the conviction that I must leave at once and go to the island of Bernera, where I found myself within three days! Almost immediately on arriving, I was in the midst of a most blessed movement. Again the promise was being fulfilled, 'I will pour water upon him that is thirsty and floods upon the dry ground'. The first few meetings were very ordinary, but the prayers offered by elders of the congregation breathed a confidence in the sure promise of God. Again and again reference was made to the words of Psalm 50, verse 3, 'Our God shall surely come'. They did not wait long for the fulfillment of this word from God! One evening, just as the congregation was leaving the church and moving down towards the main road, the Spirit of God fell upon the people in Pentecostal power: no other word can describe it: and in a few minutes the awareness of the presence of the Most High became so wonderful and so subduing, that one could only say with Jacob of old, 'Surely the Lord is in this place'. There, under the open heavens and by the road side, the voice of prayer was mingled with the groans of penitent, as 'free grace awoke men with light from on high'. Soon the whole island was in the grip of a mighty movement of the Spirit, bringing deep conviction of sin and a hunger for God. This movement was different from that in Lewis in this respect, that while in Lewis there were physical manifestations and prostrations, such were not witnessed here; but the work was as deep and the result as enduring, as in any other part touched by the revival.

Perhaps the most outstanding feature in this part of Harris

was the awe-inspiring sense of the presence of God that came over the island. The people just gave themselves to seeking the way of life. Meetings were held during the day and through the night, in church, in the homes of the people and in the open: indeed, every gathering of people was made a means of grace. One would like to pay tribute to two ministers of the Church of Scotland who, in the spirit of self-sacrifice, left their own parishes and threw their full weight into the movement, the Rev Murdo McLeod of Tarbert, and the Rev Angus McKillop of Lochs: the good people of this island will forever be grateful to those two gentlemen who gave of their best. Here is an extract from a letter received from an elder on the Island: he is referring to the first communion after the awakening: 'The centre of the church was reserved for communicants, but it could not hold them; this never happened in the history of our parish before, "Glory to God, Hallelujah"!'

The other Bernera also, in Lewis, is one of the smaller islands of the outer Hebrides, with a population of about 400 fairly equally divided between the Church of Scotland and the Free Church of Scotland. Here God had a few faithful men and women, but a long vacancy in one of the churches did not help the spiritual life of the community, and this was reflected in a growing disregard for public worship, especially by the youth of the island. It has been said that the weekly prayer meeting indicates the spiritual temperature of a congregation, and if that be so, Bernera had a somewhat low temperature: but there had been indications of the working of the Holy Spirit, and here also God and His 'Daniels' with their 'windows . . . open toward Jerusalem', who, long before the outbreak of the revival, were encouraged to believe that days of spiritual refreshing were near at hand.

One of the outstanding personalities of the revival, the Rev Murdo McLennan, Parish minister of Carloway, was Interim Moderator of the Bernera congregation. At his invitation I went to assist at a communion season and began a series of pre-communion services. The first meeting was not encouraging, and it was decided to have a further meeting in a nearby cottage. If the first meeting damped our spirits, here was a sight to gladden our hearts: a crowded house, with young men and women in the majority, and an awareness of God that was most subduing. That night in this cottage God made bare His arm, and a movement broke out that was to spread all over the island. It was here that an incident occurred that lives most vividly in my memory: at my request several office-bearers from the Parish Church of Barvas visited the island bringing with them a young lad recently brought to a saving knowledge of the truth. After spending some time together in prayer, we went to the church to find the place crowded, but seldom did I experience such bondage of spirit, and preaching was most difficult; so much so, that when only half-way through my address I stopped preaching. Just then my eye caught sight of this young lad, who was visibly moved and appeared to be deeply burdened: leaning over the pulpit I said, 'Donald, will you lead us in prayer?' There was an immediate response, and in that moment the flood-gates of Heaven opened, the congregation was struck by a hurricane of divine power, and many cried out for mercy.

But the most remarkable feature of this gracious visitation was not what happened in the church, but the spiritual impact made upon the island: men who until then had no thought of seeking after God, were suddenly arrested and became deeply concerned about their souls' salvation. One worthy elder of the Free Church into whose home salvation came, referring to his native village, said: 'This is the Lord's doing. His great name be praised'. A contributor to the local paper in an article referring to this movement wrote, 'More are attending the weekly prayer meetings than attended public worship on the Sabbath, before the revival'. It was my privilege to pay a return visit to this island, and what a joy it was to find the young converts growing in grace, and witnessing in church and community a good confession: to listen to their words of testimony or to hear them engage in prayer was 'as cold waters to a thirsty soul'.

The last place to be mentioned in connection with the spread of the movement is the Parish of Uig. This part of the island is sparsely populated, with the villages far apart, and not too well provided with transport facilities, but if buses were not available, vans and lorries were, and in these the people of the scattered townships gathered. At the beginning of the revival, while God was moving mightily in the Parish of Ness, a woman who was bitterly opposed to the movement made the remark, 'Why does He not go to Uig? That is where they need the gospel'. If by inference this lady meant that Uig was lacking in a gospel ministry, she was, I fear, using her imagination without reference to fact. Uig for many years had been favoured by a faithful and evangelical ministry. It is true that, in common with many other parishes, a spirit of indifference to the things of God prevailed, especially among the young, so that the church was supported largely by the middle-aged and old. But the faithful ministry from the pulpits, and the prevailing prayers of the people of God in the parish, did not pass the notice of Him who said, 'I will yet for this be enquired of by the house of Israel, to do it for them'.

I wish I could describe the scene, and impart something of the overwhelming sense of the subduing Spirit of God on the night that the windows of heaven opened. The parish minister, the Rev Angus MacFarlane, was in his own pulpit and was leading in prayer, when suddenly a consciousness of God came over the congregation, and we were lifted out of the realm of the ordinary, to realise a spiritual impact that could not be explained from any human point of view: revival had come. The first meeting of the evening concluded with the singing of Psalm 147, verses 2–3:

'God doth build up Jerusalem;
      And He it is alone
That the dispersed of Israel
      doth gather into one.

'Those that are broken in their heart,
　　and grieved in their minds,
He healeth, and their painful wounds
　　He tenderly up-binds.'

The second meeting of this memorable night was held in a neighbouring village. All lorries and vans available were put into service to convey people to the place of worship, yet many were forced to walk miles; but distance did not matter, and at any rate they knew that the meetings would continue: if they were not in time for the first, they would be sure of getting the second or the third. So they came across the moors and over the hills, young men and maidens, their torches flashing in the darkness, intent upon one thing, to get peace from a guilty conscience, and refuge from the storm in their bosom, in the shelter of the Rock of Ages.

Today, in this parish, the churches are throbbing with young life and the work and witness of the respective congregations made so much easier, through the new influx of men and women ready and willing to serve their Master and the church of their fathers.

Features of the Movement. What have been the outstanding features of this movement? Three stand out clearly. First an awareness of God. To be fully realised this has to be felt. A rector of the Church of England, referring to his visit to Lewis, said, 'What I felt, apart from what I saw, convinced me at once that this was no ordinary movement'. I have known men out on the fields, others at their weaving looms, so overcome by this sense of God that they were found prostrate on the ground. Here are the words of one who felt the hand of God upon him: 'The grass beneath my feet and the rocks around me seem to cry, "Flee to Christ for mercy".' This supernatural illumination of the Holy Spirit led many in this revival to a saving knowledge of the Lord Jesus Christ before they came near to any meeting connected with the movement. I have no hesitation in saying that this awareness of God is the cying need of the church today; 'The fear of the Lord is the beginning of wisdom'; but this cannot be worked up by any human effort, it must come down.

The second main feature has been deep conviction of sin – at times leading almost to despair. I have known occasions when it was necessary to stop preaching because of the distress manifested by the anxious, and many would find expression for the feeling in their hearts and the burden of their guilty conscience, in the words of John Newton:

> 'My conscience felt and owned its guilt,
>   And plunged me in despair:
> I saw my sins His Blood had spilt
>   And helped to nail Him there.

Physical manifestations and prostrations have been a further feature. I find it somewhat difficult to explain this aspect, indeed I cannot; but this I will say, that the person who would associate this with satanic influence is coming perilously near committing the unpardonable sin. Lady Huntingdon on one occasion wrote to George Whitfield respecting cases of crying out and falling down in meetings, and advised him not to remove them from the meetings, as had been done. When this was done it seemed to bring a damper on the meeting. She said, 'You are making a great mistake. Don't be wiser than God. Let them cry out; it will do a great deal more good than your preaching'.

Conclusion. Much has been said and written about the revival. Like all such movements of the past, many have praised God for it, others have made it the occasion of bitter press and pulpit attacks. 'Men have praised or blamed as it suited them.' It is true, however, that exaggerated statements have appeared in the press carrying such lines as 'Revival sweeping the Hebrides'. Revival has not swept the Hebrides: there are many parts of the Western Isles still untouched by the movement. But it is true to say that Lewis and Harris have experienced 'times of refreshing . . . from the presence of the

Lord', and the wilderness has been made to 'rejoice and blossom as the rose'.

One very much regrets that, from the beginning, there were those who opposed the movement. Here, I would quote from one who, though mightily used of God, did not escape the bitter opposition of leaders in the church: 'I verily believe revival would have come to . . . at that time if prayerful sympathy, instead of carnal criticism, had been shown'. As in this case, so also in Lewis, criticism was based on hearsay – never a wise procedure. If only those who opposed had gone to hear for themselves, how different the story might have been today! But facts are powerful things and we can leave the facts of the Lewis Revival to speak for themselves.

In 1952 the following report in 'The Scotsman' affords a good commentary of the work in Lewis:

'The Presbytery of Lewis has been holding a conference this week, and it has been attended by the Moderator of the General Assembly of the Church of Scotland, the Right Rev Dr George Johnstone Jeffrey. It has been so successful that a special open-air service was held in Percival Square, the first time that the Church of Scotland has held an open-air service in Stornoway. A children's meeting at the conference was so popular that another meeting had to be held.' At a meeting in Edinburgh on his return, the Moderator made reference with much warmth of feeling to his recent visit to Lewis and to the evangelistic zeal and fervour of the people.

God has worked and we give Him the glory.